Fantastically FUN CROSSWORDS for Kids

Trip Payne

Sterling Publishing Co., Inc.
New York

Dedicated, as always, to Brian Dominy.

Other books by Trip Payne:

Crosswords for Kids
Great Crosswords for Kids
Super Crosswords for Kids
Challenging Crosswords for Kids
Clever Crosswords for Kids
Awesome Crosswords for Kids
Amazing Crosswords for Kids

Pop Culture Crosswords
Crosswords to Strain Your Brain
Mighty Mini Crosswords
365 Celebrity Crypto-Quotes
The Little Giant Encyclopedia of Word Puzzles (co-author)

2 4 6 8 10 9 7 5 3 1

Published by Sterling Publishing Co., Inc.
387 Park Avenue South, New York, NY 10016

Distributed in Canada by Sterling Publishing
c/o Canadian Manda Group, 165 Dufferin Street
Toronto, Ontario, Canada M6K 3H6
Distributed in the United Kingdom by GMC Distribution Services
Castle Place, 166 High Street, Lewes, East Sussex, England BN7 1XU
Distributed in Australia by Capricorn Link (Australia) Pty. Ltd.
P.O. Box 704, Windsor, NSW 2756, Australia

Manufactured in the United States of America

Sterling ISBN-13: 978-1-4027-2163-2
ISBN-10: 1-4027-2163-3

For information about custom editions, special sales, premium and corporate purchases, please contact Sterling Special Sales Department at 800-805-5489 or specialsales@sterlingpub.com.

CONTENTS

INTRODUCTION

Do you like surprises?

That's one fun thing about crosswords—you never know what to expect. It's not like in school, where in math class you know you're going to get questions about math, and in history class you know you're going to get questions about history. In a crossword you have to be ready for anything. The words in a single puzzle might be about sports, food, movies—anything at all!

And the same word might be clued in completely different ways from one puzzle to the next. BAT might be the flying animal in one puzzle and the thing used by a hitter in baseball in another, so watch your step!

So if you're ready, then turn the page and dig in!

—Trip Payne

PUZZLES

1

ACROSS

1 Use scissors
4 Where you go to sleep
7 Person who rides a motorcycle
12 Country south of Canada: Abbreviation
13 How military people say "yes"
14 Not dead
15 100 of them equal 26-Across
17 "A Boy ___ Charlie Brown"
18 Receives
19 Where the sun and moon are
20 5,280 feet
22 What a lawyer charges
23 Distress signal
26 It has George Washington's face on it: 3 words
30 Magazine that features a fold-in back cover
31 The fifth month of the year
32 Raggedy ___ (boy doll)
33 "For ___ a jolly good fellow ..."
34 Say that something bad could happen
36 It's at the end of a fable
39 20 of them equal 26-Across
42 Be ___ of (know about)
43 What's left in a fireplace after a fire
44 ___ de Janeiro (city in Brazil)
45 "Don't ___ me!" ("I might do what you're saying!")
46 "Golly!"
47 Secret agent

DOWN

1 You drink out of it
2 ___ up (totally finish)
3 All snarled up
4 The worm on a fishhook, for example
5 Parts of the face
6 ___ Moines (city in Iowa)
7 The person who handles the money in Monopoly
8 "Now ___ me down to sleep": 2 words
9 "___ Possible" (TV cartoon show)

10 Adam's wife, in the Bible
11 The color of a tomato
16 Require
19 Large body of water
20 ___ and Dad
21 Once ___ while (sometimes): 2 words
22 Ride in an airplane
23 People who do wrong
24 Ancient
25 Sneaky, like a fox
27 Food that might include eggs and cheese
28 ___ Vegas
29 Sound a dog makes
33 Large stringed instrument
34 Intelligent
35 Pain
36 Welcome ___ (item outside the front door)
37 Have a debt to repay
38 Male sheep
39 Old horse
40 Part of the mouth
41 Sauce used in Chinese restaurants

2

ACROSS

1 "American ___" (music talent show)
5 "___ upon a time ..."
9 Joint near the middle of the body
12 Something you're not supposed to do: Hyphenated
13 Place to keep chickens
14 Ginger ___ (kind of drink)
15 Cartoonist who created "Peanuts": 2 words
18 "___ good turn daily" (Boy Scout slogan): 2 words
19 Animated character
20 "___ my pleasure"
23 Explosive stuff: Abbreviation
25 Sum
28 Sleep in a tent
30 Observe
32 Store where people buy meat
33 Joints in the legs
35 Short sleep
37 "Why ___ the chicken cross the road?"
38 Heavy gray metal
40 Take a small drink
42 Cartoonist who created "Calvin and Hobbes": 2 words
48 Card with one spot on it
49 One of the Great Lakes
50 State whose capital is Columbus
51 Fire truck's color
52 Bambi, for example
53 What snow will do when the weather gets warmer

DOWN

1 "Monsters, ___" (animated movie)
2 Homer Simpson's exclamation
3 Put ___ happy face (smile): 2 words
4 "Little ___ Fauntleroy" (kids' book)
5 The Atlantic and the Pacific
6 Negative answers
7 Price
8 Part of Walt Disney World
9 Like some Halloween houses
10 Sick

11 Candy that comes in its own dispenser
16 Parking ___ (place for cars)
17 It covers the engine of a car
20 "This tastes gross!"
21 Light brown
22 Took a sniff
24 Five times two
26 "___ Baba and the Forty Thieves"
27 Jar covering
29 The part of a banana you don't eat
31 Holiday with eggs and bunnies
34 Sliced a piece of wood
36 Dessert that has a crust
39 Truth or ___ (game)
41 Dance for high school students
42 Candy ___ (sweet treat)
43 Frozen water
44 Make a knot
45 That girl
46 Kind of fuel
47 "Last but ___ least ..."

3

ACROSS

1 Automobile
4 Bratty kid
7 Football team from Indianapolis
12 Gorilla
13 "Cross my heart and hope to ___"
14 Big city in Nebraska
15 A camper might use it for shelter: 2 words
17 Dug for gold
18 A magician might pull a rabbit out of it
19 Catcher's glove
20 Strings on shoes
23 One of the Seven Dwarfs
24 Female sheep
27 "___ Read With My Eyes Shut!" (Dr. Seuss book): 2 words
28 "That's amazing!"
29 Dull color
30 It's filled with ink
31 Fake hair
32 "Home on the ___"
33 Skinny
35 "We need help!"
36 Take something illegally
38 A camper might use it to find directions
42 "___ you ashamed of yourself?"
43 Light ___ feather: 2 words
44 Mike and ___ (brand of candy)
45 Chain ___ (groups of restrained prisoners)
46 2,000 pounds
47 Kind of bread

DOWN

1 A dunce might have one on his head
2 Kwik-E-Mart worker, on "The Simpsons"
3 Democrat's opponent: Abbreviation
4 Thoughts
5 Place that prints money
6 Animal you keep at home
7 ___ strip
8 Leave out
9 A camper might use it for light
10 Word that begins many book titles
11 Unhappy
16 Now and ___ (once in a while)

1	2	3		4	5	6		7	8	9	10	11
12				13				14				
15			16					17				
			18				19					
20	21	22				23				24	25	26
27					28				29			
30				31				32				
		33	34				35					
36	37					38				39	40	41
42						43				44		
45						46				47		

19 Cut the grass
20 "Button your ___" ("Be quiet")
21 Good card to have in the game blackjack
22 A camper might use it to hold water
23 Canine
25 What a happy puppy's tail will do
26 The calm center of a hurricane
28 Take first prize
29 Pant
31 Becomes limp, like old flowers
32 From the capital of Italy
34 ___ up (end a phone call)
35 Just OK: Hyphenated
36 Droop
37 "___ la la" (sounds in a song)
38 Grown-up kitten
39 What you breathe
40 Where clouds are
41 "___ you later, alligator!"

4

ACROSS

1 Big ___ (kind of hamburger)
4 Cain and ___ (sons of Adam and Eve)
8 Male deer
12 Pokémon trainer
13 Be in charge of a country
14 Company that makes toy bricks
15 What you do to shoelaces
16 ___ Watson (girl who plays Hermione in the Harry Potter movies)
17 Cats like to play with it
18 The Garden of ___
20 List of food in a restaurant
22 Girl in "Little Women"
23 It's at the end of a pencil
25 Identical
27 Person who isn't trustworthy
28 Company that made the Genesis videogame system
29 Opposite of "buy"
30 Pressure
32 "Now I understand!"
33 Masking ___
35 Con game
37 Created
39 Where you might find stalagmites and stalactites
41 How to say "yes" in French
42 Like the numbers 2, 4, and 6
43 One of the five Great Lakes
44 Material that can explode: Abbreviation
45 Geeky person
46 Hide and ___
47 Used a chair

DOWN

1 First ___ (person on a ship)
2 Step ___ (move out of the way)
3 Person who stirs up support during a game
4 "Two heads ___ better than one"
5 Something depressing
6 Hunter in Looney Tunes cartoons
7 Be tilted
8 ___ as a fox

1	2	3	■	4	5	6	7	■	8	9	10	11
12			■	13				■	14			
15			■	16				■	17			
18			19	■	20			21	■	22		
■	23			24			■	25	26			■
■	■	27				■	28				■	■
■	29				■	30					31	■
32			■	33	34			■	35			36
37			38	■	39			40	■	41		
42				■	43				■	44		
45				■	46				■	47		

9 Animals that stir up support during a game: 2 words
10 Have the same opinion
11 Musical instrument that gets hit with a hammer
19 What a hammer hits
21 ___-friendly (easy to get the hang of, like some computers)
24 You put it on French fries
26 Grows older
28 ___ Wonder (famous singer)
29 Use a razor
30 Term for knocking over ten bowling pins in two tries
31 Steam room
32 Word at the end of a prayer
34 There are four of them in a deck
36 A baseball catcher wears one
38 Finish
40 "Oh no, a mouse!"

5

ACROSS

1 Christmas's month: Abbreviation
4 "Eureka!"
7 Drink quickly
11 "Well, ___ be darned!"
12 Prefix for "colon" or "finals"
14 You can water the lawn with it
15 Enjoy a winter sport
16 Person who's in charge at a school
18 ___ and cheese (tasty meal, for short)
20 It can cool down a room
21 Person who lends out books at a school
25 ___ and downs
28 Single thing
29 "And so on": Abbreviation
30 Vanish ___ thin air
31 Pay-___-view (kind of TV show)
32 Person who cleans up at a school
34 Stomach muscles, for short
35 "You've ___ to be kidding!"
36 Person who gives advice at a school
41 "This ___ stickup!": 2 words
44 Female relative
45 Great ___ (breed of dog)
46 Homer's neighbor, on "The Simpsons"
47 Experts
48 What nodding your head means
49 Fuel for a car

DOWN

1 Prefix for "like" or "respectful"
2 Animal with large antlers
3 Mountain ___ (person who goes up large hills)
4 Group that's against hurting animals: Abbreviation
5 Not him
6 "What ___ supposed to do?": 2 words
7 A beard covers it
8 Move like a rabbit
9 Country north of Mexico: Abbreviation

1	2	3	■	4	5	6	■	■	7	8	9	10
11			■	12			13	■	14			
15			■	16				17				
■	■	18	19		■	■	20			■	■	■
21	22				23	24			■	25	26	27
28				■	29			■	30			
31			■	32				33				
■	■	■	34			■	■	35			■	■
36	37	38				39	40		■	41	42	43
44				■	45				■	46		
47				■	■	48			■	49		

10 Stuff that can make hair stay in place
13 Actually: 2 words
17 What soup comes in
19 Where the elbow is
21 It might get chapped
22 Ending for "meteor"
23 Didn't waste, in a way
24 "___ not my problem"
25 Bringing together
26 Elementary school group: Abbreviation
27 Male child
30 What a bride and groom say: 2 words
32 Network that shows "Survivor"
33 Fairy tale beasts
34 Pests at a picnic
36 Headwear for a baseball player
37 "Days of ___ Lives" (soap opera)
38 Colorful card game
39 Put down
40 Number that appears on a penny
42 The Mediterranean ___ (body of water)
43 Commercials

6

ACROSS

1 Triangle used in pool games
5 Say something untrue
8 Assistant to Captain Hook
12 Country in the Middle East
13 Poison ___ (plant that can cause a rash)
14 Items that are worn around the neck
15 ___ Le Pew
16 Peg used by a golfer
17 Forms a question
18 It might be multiple-choice
20 Cut in a skirt
22 One ___ time: 2 words
24 One of Santa's helpers
26 Black-and-white cookies
29 "What ___ know?": 2 words
30 "Cool!"
32 Queen Latifah's music
33 Tunes
35 "___ the season to be jolly ..."
36 It's up above us
37 Was sure of
39 Johnny ___ (actor in "Charlie and the Chocolate Factory")
41 The largest continent
43 Muhammad ___ (famous boxer)
45 Animal that's similar to a frog
48 ___ of (in a way)
49 "I ___ what you mean"
50 Company that Wile E. Coyote uses all the time
51 Liquids in pens
52 That lady
53 Place for a tattoo

DOWN

1 Tear
2 "You ___ My Sunshine"
3 Officer in "Star Trek": 2 words
4 Part of the leg
5 Small
6 "___ Been Working on the Railroad"
7 You see with them
8 A single step
9 Officer in "Star Trek": 2 words

1	2	3	4	■	5	6	7	■	8	9	10	11
12				■	13			■	14			
15				■	16			■	17			
■	■	18		19		■	20	21			■	■
22	23		■	24		25	■	26			27	28
29			■	30			31		■	32		
33			34		■	35			■	36		
■	■	37			38	■	39		40		■	■
41	42			■	43	44		■	45		46	47
48				■	49			■	50			
51				■	52			■	53			

10 Squealed sound

11 Ending for "lion" or "host"

19 Taste, touch, or hearing, for example

21 Not tight

22 They try to sell things

23 Also

25 Overweight

27 Tree that produces acorns

28 "Harriet the ___" (book by Louise Fitzhugh)

31 Neater

34 Pesky insects

38 Take a bath

40 School organizations: Abbreviation

41 "___ was saying ...": 2 words

42 Boy, to his parents

44 Robert E. ___ (general in the Civil War)

46 "How ___ doing?": 2 words

47 Comfortable room in the house

7

ACROSS

1 Stinging insects
6 Paddle
9 The eighth month: Abbreviation
12 Early videogame maker
13 Little white ___ (fib)
14 Country that declared independence in 1776: Abbreviation
15 "Take it easy!"
16 Puts on clothes
18 They have lids and lashes
20 Short play
21 That boy
23 Subject of a preacher's sermon
25 Small cuts
28 Spin like ___: 2 words
30 ___ Cruise (famous actor)
32 "... with my banjo on my ___" (line in "Oh! Susanna")
33 Dog that doesn't have a place to live
35 "Snow White" character
37 Sales ___ (extra amount you pay for something)
38 Lambs' mothers
40 The North ___ (where Santa lives)
42 Vehicle pulled by huskies
45 Stirs up
48 Game with "Wild Draw 4" cards
49 Zodiac sign whose symbol is a lion
50 Remove pencil marks
51 ___ Quayle (George Bush's vice president)
52 Approves
53 One of the five senses

DOWN

1 The Civil ___
2 Had a meal
3 U.S. state capital: 2 words
4 Say grace, for example
5 High numbers on dice
6 ___ King Cole
7 ___ out (freshens in the breeze)
8 Smells awful
9 U.S. state capital: 2 words
10 "What's the ___?" ("What difference will it make?")

1	2	3	4	5	■	6	7	8	■	9	10	11
12					■	13			■	14		
15					■	16			17			
■	■	18			19	■	20				■	■
21	22		■	23		24	■	25			26	27
28			29	■	30		31	■	32			
33				34	■	35		36	■	37		
■	■	38			39	■	40		41		■	■
42	43					44	■	45			46	47
48			■	49			■	50				
51			■	52			■	53				

11 ___ station (place to buy fuel)
17 Where to wash your hands
19 Command to a dog
21 "How long ___ this been going on?"
22 Cousin ___ (character in "The Addams Family")
24 Show agreement
26 "The Princess and the ___" (fairy tale)
27 Gender
29 What cats walk on
31 It's used to clean a floor
34 Mello ___ (soft drink)
36 One of Santa's reindeer
39 Look for
41 Money that was used in Italy until 2002
42 Bomb that doesn't go off
43 "Humpty Dumpty sat ___ wall": 2 words
44 Two, in Spanish
46 Suffix that means "most"
47 "Peekaboo, I ___ you!"

8

ACROSS

1 Porky is one
4 "Under the ___" (song from "The Little Mermaid")
7 Device that police use to catch speeders
12 "Now playing ___ theater near you": 2 words
13 ___ Solo (character in "Star Wars")
14 Got out of bed
15 Where someone keeps their automobile
17 Chill out
18 They're worn with men's suits
19 Breakfast, lunch, or dinner
20 Feels pain
22 Card game for two people
23 Word of agreement
26 Boats that go underwater
27 Finish a lowercase "i"
28 Small argument
29 ___ Majesty (how people refer to the Queen)
30 Animal in a dairy
31 Casual conversations
32 Long, skinny musical instrument
34 Not rich
35 Greeted the villain
37 Junk that's all over the place
40 Joint near the foot
41 It makes a canoe move
42 What O means in "I.O.U."
43 Students study for them
44 Stuff that can cause an explosion: Abbreviation
45 Mr. Flanders, on "The Simpsons"

DOWN

1 ___-Man (early videogame)
2 "Give ___ rest!": 2 words
3 Popular male country singer: 2 words
4 Sneakers or moccasins
5 Rabbits have long ones
6 Small insect
7 Less common
8 Place
9 Popular female country singer: 2 words
10 Dumb ___ rock: 2 words
11 Tyrannosaurus ___ (kind of dinosaur)

16 Desserts that might have fruit fillings
19 What wrestlers wrestle on
20 ___ Wednesday (first day of Lent)
21 Stick used by a pool player
22 "That's really something!"
24 Munch on
25 Roads and avenues: Abbreviation
27 Female deer
28 Fired a gun
30 Secret messages
31 Where a trial takes place
33 It holds pants up
34 Scheme
35 Animal that hangs upside-down in a cave
36 Eleven minus ten
37 Simple bed used by a camper
38 Female animal on a farm
39 Cherry's color

9

ACROSS

1 They add light to a room
6 Container that might have a cork in the top
9 "Crime does not ___"
12 One more time
13 Had a snack
14 ___ cream sandwich
15 Not better
16 Baseball team from New York
18 Small songbird
20 "The Little Red ___" (story)
21 "What a good boy ___!" (what Little Jack Horner said): 2 words
23 Money left for a waiter
25 Tender, achy spots
29 Piece of music
31 Pooch
33 How you might order fast food: 2 words
34 Man from ancient Greece who wrote fables
36 Stay ___ (don't move)
38 Corn on the ___
39 It's used to catch fish
41 You pour it on cereal
43 Baseball team from California
47 Puts a worm on a hook
50 Half of two
51 "Let sleeping dogs ___"
52 Important happening
53 What a sunbather might get
54 Female pig
55 Yummy

DOWN

1 Against the ___ (illegal)
2 A long time ___ (in the past)
3 Baseball team from Florida
4 The Leaning Tower of ___
5 Dog in "Hägar the Horrible"
6 Bird that's often blue
7 Its capital is Salt Lake City
8 They determine the color of your eyes, how tall you are, etc.
9 Boston cream ___
10 Card that has an A in the corner
11 Not "no" or "maybe"
17 A Boy Scout might tie one

1	2	3	4	5	■	6	7	8	■	9	10	11
12					■	13			■	14		
15					■	16			17			
■	■	18			19	■	20			■	■	■
21	22		■	23		24	■	25		26	27	28
29			30	■	31		32	■	33			
34				35	■	36		37	■	38		
■	■	■	39		40	■	41		42		■	■
43	44	45				46	■	47			48	49
50			■	51			■	52				
53			■	54			■	55				

19 Child
21 Big ___ house: 2 words
22 One of the Three Stooges
24 Rice Krispies sound
26 Baseball team from Colorado
27 A vain person has a big one
28 Cry loudly
30 Instrument that makes a loud, deep sound
32 Chewing ___
35 The skins of bananas
37 Land that wants to be independent of China
40 Group of three
42 What comes out of a volcano
43 Small circle
44 Go ___ diet: 2 words
45 Where lions live
46 Use a needle and thread
48 It's used to blow things up: Abbreviation
49 Pig pen

10

ACROSS

1 Not to mention
5 Droops down in the middle
9 Comfortable room of the house
12 Girl in "Little Women"
13 Something to avoid doing: Hyphenated
14 "___ got an idea!"
15 Villain in 29-Across: 2 words
17 Do needlework
18 Exclamation like "Aha!"
19 Pin the ___ on the donkey
21 "No ___, ands, or buts"
24 Hairy jungle animal
26 One of Columbus's three ships
29 He wrote about "A Series of Unfortunate Events"
33 What Jack Sprat's wife couldn't eat
34 Stop standing
35 A modest person has a small one
36 Bad weather for a picnic
39 It's more than "-er"
41 Kind of rodent
43 He played 15-Across on film: 2 words
48 "___ only as directed" (words on a medicine bottle)
49 A soccer player might strike a soccer ball with it
50 Midwest state
51 ___ mitzvah (ceremony for a Jewish boy)
52 Allows
53 Verse

DOWN

1 Start of the alphabet
2 One of the signs of the zodiac
3 Name that sounds like "stew"
4 "How awful!": 2 words
5 Charlie Brown's dog
6 Computer service with Buddy List and Instant Messages: Abbreviation
7 Annoying insect
8 Furniture in the living room
9 Don't enjoy
10 Christmas ___ (December 24)
11 ___ York City
16 "Easier said ___ done"

1	2	3	4	■	5	6	7	8	■	9	10	11
12				■	13				■	14		
15				16					■	17		
■	■	■	18			■	19		20		■	■
21	22	23	■	24		25	■	■	26		27	28
29			30				31	32				
33				■	■	34			■	35		
■	■	36		37	38	■	39		40	■	■	■
41	42		■	43		44				45	46	47
48			■	49				■	50			
51			■	52				■	53			

20 "Monsters, ___"
21 Not feeling well
22 What something costs
23 More intelligent
25 Ending for "count" or "priest"
27 Opposite of "positive": Abbreviation
28 From ___ Z (completely): 2 words
30 Like a bump ___ log: 2 words
31 Certain female relatives
32 "___ small world after all": 2 words
37 Letters between H and M
38 Three times three
40 Journey
41 ___ the wrong way (irritate)
42 Proud ___ peacock: 2 words
44 "You've ___ your match!"
45 Kanga's kid, in "Winnie-the-Pooh"
46 Female animal with wool
47 Sweet potato

11

ACROSS

1 "In ___ We Trust" (motto on U.S. money)
4 Taxis
8 Father of a fawn
12 King Kong, for example
13 Above
14 Where you live
15 Yellow property in Monopoly: 2 words
18 Large lake near Pennsylvania
19 Cats chase them
20 Suffix for "baron" or "heir"
21 Less able to walk easily
23 Member of Congress: Abbreviation
24 "___ you later!"
25 Broken-down horse
27 Answer to an addition problem
29 You might stand on one after a bath
32 Make an offer at an auction
34 Bats use it to determine locations
38 "How was ___ know?": 2 words
39 What a fisherman uses to attract fish
41 Host of "The Tonight Show"
42 Yellow property in Monopoly: 2 words
45 Something ___ (not this)
46 All the ___ (constantly)
47 "If I should ___ before I wake ..."
48 The opening in a piggy bank that you put the coins into
49 A ___ in the right direction
50 "Definitely!"

DOWN

1 A judge pounds it
2 Soap ___ (kind of TV show)
3 Material that jeans are made from
4 "You ___ do it!"
5 Part of a molecule
6 ___ and Natasha (villains on "Rocky and Bullwinkle")
7 ___ out (stops paying attention)

1	2	3	■	4	5	6	7	■	8	9	10	11
12			■	13				■	14			
15			16					17				
18				■	19				■	20		
21				22	■	23			■	24		
■	■	■	25		26	■	27		28	■	■	■
29	30	31	■	32		33	■	34		35	36	37
38			■	39			40	■	41			
42			43					44				
45				■	46				■	47		
48				■	49				■	50		

8 This woman
9 Dial ___ (sounds on telephones)
10 Entertain
11 Birds that fly in a V shape
16 Kid between 12 and 20 years old
17 The second planet from the Sun
22 Jewish religious leader
26 San Francisco baseball team
28 It grows on old bread
29 They entertain people without talking
30 Not ___ (not a bit): 2 words
31 Upper part of the body
33 Number
35 Poor
36 Little Orphan ___
37 Red flowers
40 Not wild
43 Doctor for animals
44 Member of Congress who isn't a senator: Abbreviation

12

ACROSS

1 Talk a lot
4 Toboggan
8 One of the Three Bears
12 "___ your head!" ("Don't be stupid!")
13 Heap
14 Middle-___ (not young or old)
15 Classic sitcom about George and Louise: 2 words
18 Small number
19 Large airplane
20 Responded to applause from the audience
23 Magazine featuring Alfred E. Neuman
24 ___ code (number on an envelope)
27 Run ___ (leave home)
28 ___ attention (listen carefully)
29 It ebbs and flows
30 Dallas's state: Abbreviation
31 Half a dozen
32 Someone who teaches people one at a time
33 What's inside a football
34 King ___ (old Egyptian Pharaoh)
35 Classic sitcom about a large family: 3 words
42 Cain's brother, in the Bible
43 Cassette
44 Ghost's word
45 Totem ___ (tribal symbol)
46 Body parts that blink
47 Kind of animal that Tarzan hung out with

DOWN

1 Belly
2 What's left after something is burned
3 Insect that makes honey
4 Use cash
5 "Variety is the spice of ___"
6 Magical being
7 Someone who plays songs on the radio
8 Not the present or future
9 "Many years ___ ..."
10 Ballpoint ___
11 They interrupt TV shows
16 Baby kangaroo
17 Main color of a stop sign

1	2	3	■	4	5	6	7	■	8	9	10	11
12			■	13				■	14			
15			16					17				
■	■	■	18			■	19			■	■	■
20	21	22			■	23			■	24	25	26
27				■	28			■	29			
30			■	31			■	32				
■	■	■	33			■	34			■	■	■
35	36	37				38				39	40	41
42				■	43				■	44		
45				■	46				■	47		

20 The only mammal that flies
21 "I ___ you one!" ("I'm in your debt!")
22 A candle is made from it
23 The Grinch's pet dog
24 Pimple
25 Words at a wedding: 2 words
26 Miles ___ hour
28 Blackbeard or Long John Silver
29 Skirt worn by a ballerina
31 What Marcie calls Peppermint Patty
32 Toothpaste containers
33 Ready, willing, and ___
34 Use a keyboard
35 Noisy kind of dancing
36 Cable channel that shows lots of movies
37 Long, skinny fish
38 24 hours
39 The Chicago Bulls are in it: Abbreviation
40 Police officer
41 Gardener's tool

13

ACROSS

1 Damage
5 Not good
8 American soldiers
11 Get frosty, like winter roads: 2 words
13 Manjula's husband, on "The Simpsons"
14 New Year's ___
15 Rival of Coke
16 Boy's name that's a room of the house backward
17 Drink that contains caffeine
18 Sounds of laughter: 2 words
20 It might be pierced
22 ___ of soap (something to get clean with)
25 Some religious women
27 Take a nap
30 Rich, brown dessert: 2 words
33 Information for a computer
34 A ___ "apple": 2 words
35 Pinocchio's nose grew when he told one
36 Cost an ___ and a leg
38 Animal that's chased by another animal
40 Fast plane
42 Slippery fish
44 "Of course you realize this ___ war" (Bugs Bunny line)
48 Have debts
49 "___ always say ...": 2 words
50 "___-dabba-doo!"
51 "That's right!"
52 Permit
53 Look through a book

DOWN

1 Really cool
2 Card that can be worth 1 or 11
3 George W. Bush's party: Abbreviation
4 What you say to make sled dogs go
5 Dessert with fruit and ice cream: 2 words
6 Relative of a baboon
7 ___ ranch (Western place)
8 "Be serious!": 2 words

1	2	3	4	■	■	5	6	7	■	8	9	10
11				12	■	13			■	14		
15					■	16			■	17		
■	■	■	18		19		■	20	21		■	■
22	23	24	■	25			26	■	27		28	29
30			31					32				
33				■	34				■	35		
■	■	36		37	■	38			39	■	■	■
40	41		■	42	43		■	44		45	46	47
48			■	49			■	50				
51			■	52			■	■	53			

9 "___ had it!"
10 Caribbean ___ (big body of water)
12 Musical instrument that has 88 keys
19 Hawaiian dance
21 Part of a circle
22 Letters before E
23 "Now I get it!"
24 Spins
26 Move a muscle
28 Water-___ (have fun on a lake)
29 It holds up a golf ball
31 Means of transportation
32 Foe
37 Lunch, for one
39 Twelve months
40 "___ to the World" (Christmas carol)
41 Ram's mate
43 Suffix for "Vietnam"
45 President Lincoln's nickname
46 Miami Heat's organization: Abbreviation
47 Downhearted

14

ACROSS

1 ___ Penn (famous actor)
5 Billboards, for example
8 Long-lasting hair wave
12 Brand of frozen waffles
13 What a ram says
14 The largest continent
15 President from 1913 to 1921: 2 words
18 When the sun is out
19 Thanksgiving vegetable
20 Woolly animal
23 It's at the bottom of a skirt
24 Drumstick
27 "___ your horses!"
28 It might be in a garage
29 Candy ___ (red-and-white treat)
30 Sound of fright
31 Class where you make drawings
32 Avoid a thrown ball, in a playground game
33 "What can ___ to help?": 2 words
34 Sound from a cow
35 President from 1829 to 1837: 2 words
42 Toy that goes up and down on a string: Hyphenated
43 Polka ___ (circle on a fabric)
44 Coin that replaced the German mark
45 Not odd
46 "Monkey ___, monkey do"
47 Grown-up fawn

DOWN

1 Homophone of "so"
2 A self-centered person has a large one
3 A while ___ (in the past)
4 Indicated agreement
5 "It's ___!" (what a nurse might tell a new father): 2 words
6 "See-saw, Margery ___ ..."
7 Tom ___ (Mark Twain hero)
8 Tree that's common in Florida
9 Suffix for "lion"
10 ___ Grande (river in Texas)
11 What a boy will become
16 Music by OutKast
17 Sam-___ ("Green Eggs and Ham" character): Hyphenated

1	2	3	4	■	5	6	7	■	8	9	10	11
12				■	13			■	14			
15				16				17				
■	■	■	18			■	19			■	■	■
20	21	22			■	23			■	24	25	26
27				■	28			■	29			
30			■	31			■	32				
■	■	■	33			■	34			■	■	■
35	36	37				38				39	40	41
42				■	43			■	44			
45				■	46			■	47			

20 "But when ___ got there, the cupboard was bare ..."
21 Tool used in a garden
22 Moose
23 Frosty the Snowman wore one
24 Boy
25 London's country: Abbreviation
26 "___ whiz!"
28 Mobs of people
29 Made dinner
31 Ending for "lemon" or "lime"
32 Friend of Sneezy and Sleepy
33 Get wrinkles out of clothes
34 The end of a chess game
35 "Yes," to a sailor
36 Thanksgiving's month: Abbreviation
37 Color Easter eggs
38 Frank's brother, in the Hardy Boys books
39 Take someone to court
40 State next to California: Abbreviation
41 Neither this ___ that

15

ACROSS

1 "Well, obviously!"
4 Unexpected problem
8 Ocean liner, for example
12 "Birds ___ feather flock together": 2 words
13 Deal with
14 Area ___ (part of a phone number)
15 It comes out of a shower: 2 words
17 From ___ (totally): 3 words
18 "You ___ what you eat"
19 Take a ___ (get clean)
21 Feeling pain
24 Amount at an auction
25 Place for a hearing aid
28 Friend of Winnie-the-Pooh
29 Have three square ___ a day
31 Had a feast
32 Little baby
33 ___ conditioning
34 First man in the Bible
35 "I ___ care!"
37 Brother's sibling, for short
39 In the near future
41 Very successful people
46 Encourage
47 Great Lake that forms part of Pennsylvania's border
48 ___ Willie Winkie
49 Filthy place
50 Hard to find
51 The ___ of gravity (scientific rule)

DOWN

1 What Homer Simpsons says when he's upset
2 Spacecraft from another planet: Abbreviation
3 "The Cat in the ___"
4 Villain in "The Lion King"
5 Short letter
6 Orangutan, for example
7 Rodent that can be kept as a pet
8 "Get out of here!"
9 Person with a short temper
10 "What will ___ now?": 2 words
11 ___ dispenser (something that ejects candy)
16 One-___ street

1	2	3	■	4	5	6	7	■	8	9	10	11
12			■	13				■	14			
15			16					■	17			
■	■	■	18			■	19	20			■	■
21	22	23		■	■	24			■	25	26	27
28			■	29	30				■	31		
32			■	33			■	■	34			
■	■	35	36			■	37	38		■	■	■
39	40			■	41	42				43	44	45
46				■	47				■	48		
49				■	50				■	51		

20 "Help wanted" notices
21 Stuff in museums
22 Pigeon's sound
23 Frankfurters
24 Chocolate ___ (Hershey's product)
26 ___ distance (far away): 2 words
27 Band led by Michael Stipe
29 Guy
30 ___ this or that
34 Stuff that's left over in a barbecue
36 The number 11 contains two of them
37 Mix by hand
38 "___ what you mean": 2 words
39 Total
40 State on the Pacific Ocean: Abbreviation
42 "Are you a man ___ mouse?": 2 words
43 Bird that hoots
44 Drink that's popular in China
45 Join with stitches

16

ACROSS

1 The Ghost of Christmas ___ (character in "A Christmas Carol")
5 The alphabet
9 Kind of evergreen
12 Brand of dog food
13 Use the telephone
14 Boise's state: Abbreviation
15 Try to lose weight
16 Thing you'd find in a forest
17 A spider has eight of them
19 Wives of rams
21 Terrible
22 Shallow ponds
24 Pennies and nickels, for example
26 What Dumbo flapped in order to fly
27 "___ yourself at home"
28 ___ Agassi (tennis player)
30 Events with marching bands and floats
33 "___ Story" (animated movie)
34 "Don't cry ___ spilled milk"
36 New ___ (state)
37 Bank offering
39 Gulps down
41 False statement
42 ___ Domini (what "A.D." stands for)
43 Word after "stomach" or "tooth"
44 Spike ___ (film director)
45 Mailed
46 Tilt to one side

DOWN

1 Lily ___ (leaf in a pond)
2 Creatures from outer space
3 Casts out, like lava from a volcano
4 Carry
5 Perform onstage
6 Small, plastic girl: 2 words
7 Not dirty
8 Winter vehicles
9 ___ in the blanks
10 Thought

■	■	■	■	1	2	3	4	■	5	6	7	8
9	10	11	■	12				■	13			
14			■	15				■	16			
17			18	■	19			20	■	21		
22				23			■	24	25			
■	■	26				■	27				■	■
28	29				■	30					31	32
33			■	34	35			■	36			
37			38	■	39			40	■	41		
42				■	43				■	44		
45				■	46				■	■	■	■

11 Small, stuffed girl: 2 words
18 Fly high
20 What you might get if you cut your skin
23 Cookie with a cream filling
25 Not too bad
27 George Washington's wife
28 Book of maps
29 Not a single person: 2 words
30 Period of calm
31 Great Lake that Cleveland is next to
32 ___-ball (game where you roll balls)
35 Meat that comes from calves
38 "Ripley's Believe It or ___!"
40 Person in Congress: Abbreviation

17

ACROSS

1 Father
4 The mad ___ party (scene in "Alice in Wonderland")
7 Rock, ___, scissors
12 ___ skating
13 The Revolutionary ___
14 ___ Oyl (Popeye's girlfriend)
15 Doctor who works on teeth
17 Lugged around
18 Suffix for "differ"
19 ___ Sajak (host of "Wheel of Fortune")
20 Notion
23 Garfield is one
24 You might use one in a treasure hunt
27 Doctor who cares for the skin
31 "Pick on somebody your ___ size!"
32 ___ the grass
33 Where Japan is
34 Something to drink from
35 Frying ___
37 Entrances in fences
40 Doctor who works in an operating room
44 By oneself
45 It's attached to the shoulder
46 Lamb's mother
47 Liquid measures
48 Not wet
49 ___ down (disappoint)

DOWN

1 "What ___ you say?"
2 High card
3 Lion's home
4 Someone whose brother or sister has the same birthday
5 Direction where the sun rises
6 State-of-the-___ (high-tech)
7 Mr. ___ Head (toy)
8 Many: 2 words
9 The center of a cherry
10 The night before a holiday, like Christmas
11 ___ Rover (playground game)
16 Group of athletes
19 Buddy
20 What people say when they get married: 2 words

1	2	3	■	4	5	6	■	7	8	9	10	11
12			■	13			■	14				
15			16				■	17				
■	■	■	18			■	19			■	■	■
20	21	22		■	■	23			■	24	25	26
27				28	29				30			
31			■	32			■	■	33			
■	■	■	34			■	35	36		■	■	■
37	38	39			■	40				41	42	43
44					■	45			■	46		
47					■	48			■	49		

21 Mountain ___ (soft drink)
22 Ending for "north" or "south"
23 Animal that gives milk
24 Prefix for "fortune" or "understanding"
25 "It's just ___ thought!": 2 words
26 Group that might hold an open house: Abbreviation
28 Makes other people laugh
29 From ___ to bottom
30 Group of kids who hang out together
34 Word on a penny
35 Happy cat's sound
36 Branch of the military
37 Space between two teeth
38 "Prince ___" (song from "Aladdin")
39 Heavy weight
40 Depressed
41 Electric ___ (kind of fish)
42 Homophone of "oh"
43 It's on a basketball hoop

18

ACROSS

1 Capital of Oregon
6 ___ Kim (rapper)
9 Sack
12 Still breathing
13 "Where ___?" (lost person's question): 2 words
14 ___ down (get into bed)
15 Went out with
16 Touch gently, as with a washcloth
17 Where the funny bone is
18 You can catch a mouse in one
20 Animal that's similar to an alligator, for short
22 San Francisco's state: Abbreviation
24 "Thanks a ___!"
26 It's near the bottom of the leg
29 Made a picture
31 Sound of a punch
33 One of Adam and Eve's sons
34 Stitched
36 Item in Dora the Explorer's backpack
38 What some people say when they see a mouse
39 Woodwind instrument
41 ___ McEntire (country singer)
43 It's like jelly
45 Letters between T and X
47 Donald ___ (businessman on "The Apprentice")
50 Private ___ (detective)
51 Take a look at
52 "Peter, Peter, pumpkin ___ ..."
53 One plus two plus three plus four
54 Conclusion
55 Out of ___ (no longer popular)

DOWN

1 Down in the dumps
2 Pie ___ mode: 2 words
3 Book about the March girls: 2 words
4 "And they lived happily ___ after"
5 Gold ___ (what a winner might receive)
6 Young boy
7 Colorful Apple computer
8 Sign of the zodiac whose symbol is the scales

1	2	3	4	5	■	6	7	8	■	9	10	11
12					■	13			■	14		
15					■	16			■	17		
■	■	18			19	■	20		21		■	■
22	23		■	24		25	■	26			27	28
29			30	■	31		32	■	33			
34				35	■	36		37	■	38		
■	■	39			40	■	41		42		■	■
43	44		■	45		46	■	47			48	49
50			■	51			■	52				
53			■	54			■	55				

9 Book about a horse: 2 words
10 We all need it to live
11 Jewel
19 Soda ___
21 Go ___ vacation: 2 words
22 They hold music: Abbreviation
23 "Roses ___ red ..."
25 "The piper's son," in a nursery rhyme
27 Sara ___ (brand of frozen desserts)
28 Deer with large antlers
30 "Charlotte's ___"
32 World ___ II (battle of the 1940s)
35 Put out a fire
37 "Oh, for ___ sake!"
40 ___-steven (perfectly equal)
42 Badly behaved kid
43 You could fly in one
44 How Marines say "yes"
46 Marry
48 ___ Blanc (man who did the voice of Bugs Bunny)
49 Prefix that means "before"

19

ACROSS

1 Rival of CBS and NBC
4 "Fuzzy Wuzzy ___ a bear"
7 Continent where India is
11 Small green vegetable
12 ___ Baba
13 ___ a living (take home a paycheck)
14 Singer known as "The King of Rock and Roll": 2 words
17 What you could hear if you shouted in a canyon
18 Mother deer
19 Comfortable, like a small house
21 Chips and ___ (snack food)
22 You wipe your feet on it before entering a house
25 "When ___ your age ...": 2 words
26 It's used to hit a baseball
27 Song for one person
28 Two less than a dozen
29 When Mother's Day is
30 Bees make it
31 "You asked ___ it!"
32 Popular things that don't last long
33 Singer known as "Ol' Blue Eyes": 2 words
38 The Golden ___ ("Do unto others ...")
39 Jack ___ Jill
40 In one ___ and out the other
41 ___ child (kid with no brothers or sisters)
42 "That's true"
43 Dark-colored bread

DOWN

1 Bigger relative of a monkey
2 "The Fresh Prince of ___-Air" (Will Smith sitcom)
3 Person who lived in prehistoric times
4 Wishy-___ (going back and forth)
5 Competitor of Kal Kan
6 ___ Lancelot (famous knight)
7 Writer of "The Tortoise and the Hare"
8 When prices are marked down
9 Dublin's country: Abbreviation

1	2	3	■	4	5	6	■	7	8	9	10	■
11			■	12			■	13				■
14			15				16					■
■	■	17				■	18			■	■	■
19	20				■	21			■	22	23	24
25				■	26			■	27			
28			■	29			■	30				
■	■	■	31			■	32				■	■
■	33	34				35					36	37
■	38				■	39			■	40		
■	41				■	42			■	43		

10 "Baa, baa, black sheep, have you ___ wool?"
15 Puts frosting on
16 Work on a newspaper article
19 Punch
20 Be in debt
21 Groundhog ___ (February 2)
22 Cookie ___ ("Sesame Street" character)
23 Ginger ___
24 Plaything
26 What an angry dog might do
27 Soft drink
29 Cash
30 They're balled up to make fists
31 Autumn
32 ___ and dandy
33 To and ___
34 Move quickly
35 "You can ___ that again!"
36 X-___ vision (one of Superman's powers)
37 "A fool and his money ___ soon parted"

20

ACROSS

1 Bumper ___ (amusement park vehicles)
5 Cloth used for dusting
8 "Shoo!"
12 Blind as ___: 2 words
13 "___ not like green eggs and ham!": 2 words
14 ___ stick (bouncy toy)
15 ___ Rose (ballplayer who was banned from baseball)
16 You can buy them at a music store: Abbreviation
17 Thing
18 "The ___ of Peter Rabbit"
20 Gasp
22 The heroine in "Beauty and the Beast"
24 Ring of flowers given out in Hawaii
25 One ___ kind (unique): 2 words
28 "You ___ me one" ("I'll ask you for a favor back later")
29 Sends off
31 Todd and Rod's father, on "The Simpsons"
32 "Uh-huh"
33 Its capital is Salem: Abbreviation
34 Animals that baa
36 "That's ___ of your business!"
38 President's "no" on a bill from Congress
39 Snare
41 Number of people in a duo
43 Small blooms
46 Nature walk
47 Head covering
48 "Look ___ from my point of view": 2 words
49 Garden in the book of Genesis
50 Chopping tool
51 Those people

DOWN

1 ___ gun (toy that shoots blanks)
2 Honest ___ (Lincoln's nickname)
3 Dangerous reptile
4 What robbers do
5 It's thrown at weddings
6 Use a plus sign
7 Religious music
8 Move in circles

1	2	3	4	■	5	6	7	■	8	9	10	11
12				■	13			■	14			
15				■	16			■	17			
■	■	18		19		■	20	21			■	■
22	23				■	24			■	25	26	27
28			■	29	30				■	31		
32			■	33			■	34	35			
■	■	36	37			■	38				■	■
39	40			■	41	42		■	43		44	45
46				■	47			■	48			
49				■	50			■	51			

9 Dangerous reptile
10 How old you are
11 ___ Hanks (famous actor)
19 Sour fruit
21 What a bride walks down
22 "All work and no play makes Jack a dull ___"
23 Animal that baas
24 Tell a whopper
26 When Valentine's Day is: Abbreviation
27 Things that attempt to sell products
30 ___ Franklin (singer known as "The Queen of Soul")
35 Ready to hit, in baseball: 2 words
37 Not shut
38 Participate in an election
39 Shoot ___ breeze (chat)
40 Get ___ of (eliminate)
42 Material in candles
44 What batteries eventually do
45 Where a pig lives

21

ACROSS

1 ___ beam (part of a CD player)
6 Archenemy
9 One of the TV networks
12 Opposite of "dead"
13 Animal in the zodiac
14 "What was that you said?"
15 Thing you fold and then throw: 2 words
18 Pecan, for one
19 Blend together
20 Fishing pole
23 ___ Jersey
25 Screams
28 Oodles: 2 words
30 The ___ Hatter ("Alice in Wonderland" character)
32 Coin worth ten cents
33 Magical being who grants wishes
35 U.S. soldiers
37 Ending for "insist"
38 Length times width, for a rectangle
40 The fourth month: Abbreviation
42 Things you fill with liquid and then throw: 2 words
48 How old a person is
49 "___ tell you what ..."
50 "All that glitters ___ gold": 2 words
51 Letters used in an emergency
52 Slippery as an ___
53 ___-weeny (small)

DOWN

1 Where you put a napkin when you eat
2 State next to Georgia: Abbreviation
3 Take a small drink
4 Divisible by two
5 TV show that's been on before
6 End of the school week: Abbreviation
7 Rowing tools
8 Opposite of "full"
9 ___ Brown (character in "Peanuts")
10 What a hot dog is put into
11 "___ sells seashells by the seashore" (tongue twister)
16 "Up and ___!": 2 words

1	2	3	4	5	■	6	7	8	■	9	10	11
12					■	13			■	14		
15					16				17			
■	■	■	18			■	19				■	■
20	21	22	■	23		24	■	25			26	27
28			29	■	30		31	■	32			
33				34	■	35		36	■	37		
■	■	38			39	■	40		41	■	■	■
42	43					44				45	46	47
48			■	49			■	50				
51			■	52			■	53				

17 Wasn't honest
20 Old piece of cloth
21 What Spanish people shout at a bullfight
22 Gives to charity
24 Go back and forth, like a dog's tail
26 Letters after K
27 "Ready, ___, go!"
29 Spare ___ (item in a car's trunk)
31 Part of an old-style phone
34 Spooky
36 Banana ___ (kind of dessert)
39 Up to the job
41 Flower that has thorns
42 Used to be
43 "A long time ___, in a galaxy far, far away ..."
44 100 percent
45 Number of horns on a unicorn
46 Prefix for "violent"
47 Home for pigs

22

ACROSS

1 The Arctic or the Indian, for example
6 Sticky stuff in a maple tree
9 Young man
12 It holds a painting
13 Lemon meringue ___
14 Have to pay money to
15 Overweight cartoon star: 2 words
17 Sprinted
18 New Year's ___ (December 31)
19 "So ___ me!" (sarcastic comment)
20 Begin
22 ___ and Stimpy (cartoon pair from the 1990s)
23 ___ and ends (various things)
25 Tools that can chop down trees
26 "Hansel ___ Gretel"
27 Summer month: Abbreviation
29 Fired a gun
32 Material that people knit with
34 ___ wrestling (strength competition)
37 Pepe ___ (cartoon skunk): 2 words
39 Carpenter's tool
40 Word before "horse" or "shell"
41 "What ___ you talking about?"
42 What 15-Across was famous for saying: 3 words
45 Half of twenty
46 Yoko ___ (singer who was married to John Lennon)
47 Have a screw ___ (be crazy)
48 Suffix for "host"
49 Letters before V
50 Opposite of "higher"

DOWN

1 Have a lot to ___ (have many good qualities)
2 Strongly desire
3 Devoured
4 "I ___ bear of very little brain" (Winnie-the-Pooh quote): 2 words
5 Bully on "The Simpsons"
6 ___ limit (how fast cars are allowed to go)
7 It's in the atmosphere
8 They might need to be housebroken

1	2	3	4	5	■	6	7	8	■	9	10	11
12					■	13			■	14		
15					16				■	17		
18			■	19			■	20	21			
22			■	23			24	■	25			
■	■	■	26			■	27	28		■	■	■
29	30	31		■	32	33			■	34	35	36
37				38	■	39			■	40		
41			■	42	43				44			
45			■	46			■	47				
48			■	49			■	50				

9 Dr. Seuss character who speaks for the trees
10 Be ___ of (know about)
11 Bumps in a car's fender
16 Good pal
21 Game where you don't want to be "it"
24 ___ McLachlan (popular singer)
26 Had lunch
28 Sick
29 Last name of Fred Flintstone's boss
30 "___ mud in your eye!" (what some people say as a toast)
31 Unlocks
33 "Do ___ please": 2 words
34 Put on ___ (entertain people): 2 words
35 One of the brothers on "Malcolm in the Middle"
36 Oscar ___ (brand of lunch meat)
38 "___ That Girl?" (early Madonna song)
43 Ending for "absorb"
44 ___-Hoo (kind of chocolate drink)

23

ACROSS

1 The first three letters
4 "And others": Abbreviation
7 The Devil
12 Scooby-___
13 Pal of Tigger and Eeyore
14 Friend, in Spanish
15 Prince Charles, to Queen Elizabeth
16 At this very moment
17 Lost color, like old jeans
18 Thing at the end of a finger or toe
20 What knees do
21 Slice
23 Too big ___ one's britches
24 Room for a scientist
27 "___ upon a time ..."
28 Chicken ___ (disease)
29 Blood ___ (A, B, AB, or O)
30 Explosive used by Wile E. Coyote: Abbreviation
31 Polish a car
32 Cut wood
33 Get a grade of F
35 Transportation from the airport, sometimes
36 "You can't teach ___ dog new tricks": 2 words
38 Pistol
39 New York Knicks' group: Abbreviation
42 Put out, like a fire
43 An aardvark might eat one
44 It opens a lock
45 Mistake
46 What a lamb would say
47 Wait and ___ (don't decide immediately)

DOWN

1 TV commercials
2 Scary sound
3 Game where you try to get small disks all in a row: 2 words
4 Bert's friend, on "Sesame Street"
5 Hammer or screwdriver, for example
6 Beef comes from this animal
7 More secure
8 "As I was going to St. Ives, I met ___ with seven wives": 2 words
9 Game where you try to get small disks into a cup

1	2	3	■	4	5	6	■	7	8	9	10	11
12			■	13			■	14				
15			■	16			■	17				
■	■	18	19			■	20				■	■
21	22				■	23			■	24	25	26
27				■	28			■	29			
30			■	31			■	32				
■	■	33	34			■	35				■	■
36	37				■	38			■	39	40	41
42					■	43			■	44		
45					■	46			■	47		

10 The Ice ___ (when glaciers covered the Earth)
11 Indicate "yes" with your head
19 Card without a number or a face on it
20 Crate
21 You can boil water in it
22 Holiday ___ (hotel chain)
23 Network that shows "The Simpsons"
25 Beast from the jungle
26 Place for napping
28 Pen ___ (faraway person you write to)
29 The Internal Revenue Service collects it
31 Longer across the middle
32 Kriss Kringle's other name
34 As well
35 ___ fish sandwich
36 Ending for "Gator" or "lemon"
37 Neither here ___ there
38 The gift of ___ (the ability to speak well)
40 Insect that lives in a hive
41 How a sailor indicates agreement

24

ACROSS

1 One of the Smurfs
5 Mother
8 Go downhill on snow
11 "Fun for all ___" (words on some game boxes)
12 "What did ___ to deserve this?": 2 words
13 What a model car comes in before it's built
14 Foods that go together: 3 words
17 That woman
18 Not ___ (not so far)
19 Where Santa invites kids to sit
22 Paintings, sculptures, and so on
24 On the ___ (honest)
28 They're higher than face cards
30 Uncle ___ (symbol of the United States)
32 Rescue
33 You stick it on an envelope
35 Scratch ___ (paper to doodle on)
37 A fisherman might throw it into the water
38 "How ___ you?"
40 ___ rummy (card game)
42 Foods that go together: 3 words
48 Forest animal with antlers
49 Change the color of one's hair
50 Chicken noodle ___
51 It makes cars go
52 ___ the table (get ready for dinner)
53 ___ the Tiger (Frosted Flakes' mascot)

DOWN

1 Soft food for babies
2 In the past
3 What the P stands for in "MPH"
4 Says a question
5 They might dig for gold
6 Unusual
7 "___-Dick" (book about a whale)
8 Shoes with wheels on the bottom
9 Relatives
10 "___ about time!" ("Finally!")
15 "I get it!"

16 Slippery sea creature
19 ___ Vegas, Nevada
20 Put on an ___ (pretend)
21 Vegetable in a pod
23 ___ water (what comes out of a faucet)
25 Martin ___ Buren (former president)
26 Woman in the Garden of Eden
27 "___ me make this perfectly clear ..."
29 Cereal with the mascot Dig'Em
31 It can attract metal
34 Person who's not an amateur
36 "Look what I ___!"
39 Stops
41 Bird's home
42 Command to a dog
43 Birmingham's state: Abbreviation
44 Military way to say "yes"
45 Sticky stuff
46 BB ___ (kind of toy)
47 Someone who tries to find out secrets

25

ACROSS

1 Quick swims
5 ___ office (place to mail letters)
9 Money paid to a lawyer
12 Western state
13 Prefix that means "against"
14 Nibbled on
15 Extinct bird, or a stupid person
16 Tie score
18 "You can ___ a horse to water but you can't make him drink"
20 "Not ___ long shot!": 2 words
21 One of Christopher Robin's friends
23 Part of a minute: Abbreviation
25 Take a big drink
29 "Monsters, ___" (2001 movie)
30 Love a lot
33 Good card to have in the card game war
34 Hardwood trees
36 Grown-up puppy
37 Ham on ___ (kind of sandwich)
38 "Do you know who ___?": 2 words
41 Material that can become a diamond
43 ___ Holmes (famous detective)
47 1990s fad game involving cardboard disks
50 2,000-pound weight
51 The ___ Ranger
52 Sound at a canyon
53 "Are we having fun ___?"
54 "Money ___ everything"
55 ___ rope (use a jump rope)

DOWN

1 Firecracker that doesn't go off
2 "Who am ___ say?": 2 words
3 You use a key to open it
4 "There was an old woman who lived in a ___"
5 Like football players' uniforms
6 Six minus five
7 Pierce with a knife
8 Very neat
9 ___ Schwarz (toy store)
10 "And many others": Abbreviation
11 "That's scary!"

1	2	3	4	■	5	6	7	8	■	9	10	11
12				■	13				■	14		
15				■	16				17			
■	■	18		19		■	20			■	■	■
21	22		■	23		24	■	■	25	26	27	28
29			■	30			31	32	■	33		
34			35	■	■	36			■	37		
■	■	■	38	39	40	■	41		42		■	■
43	44	45				46		■	47		48	49
50			■	51				■	52			
53			■	54				■	55			

17 ___ Vegas (city in Nevada)

19 Stubborn ___ mule: 2 words

21 ___ de Janeiro, Brazil

22 Out ___ limb (in danger): 2 words

24 Kind of fish

26 Male witch

27 Frosty

28 "Holy cow!"

31 Bottle ___ (kind of firework)

32 A conceited person has a big one

35 Polite thing to call a man

39 "___ Want for Christmas Is My Two Front Teeth": 2 words

40 Sounds like a cow

42 "Lord of the ___" (nickname for Tarzan)

43 Place where pigs are kept

44 A gardener uses it to attack weeds

45 Ending for "depend"

46 Cable channel that focuses on news

48 Letters after F

49 ___ up (absorb, like a sponge)

26

ACROSS

1 Feature on phones that aren't touch-tone
5 Start of "The Alphabet Song"
8 Upper ___ (capital letters)
12 Dull pain
13 Sound from a calf
14 Region
15 Creator of Peter Rabbit and Squirrel Nutkin: 2 words
18 Boy, to his father
19 It shines in the sky
20 Traffic ___ (problem during rush hour)
23 ___-of-war (game)
25 Large African cat
29 Door that leads outside
31 "Please help us!"
33 Make a street smoother
34 Its capital is Austin
36 Bottom's opposite
38 Get up on the wrong side of the ___
39 Be untruthful
41 "Stuck a feather in his ___ and called it macaroni" (line from "Yankee Doodle")
43 Creator of Ramona Quimby and Henry Huggins: 2 words
50 Strong ___ ox: 2 words
51 Larry, ___, and Curly (the Three Stooges)
52 Not false
53 Place for a camper
54 Your and my
55 ___ for (summoned)

DOWN

1 Apply gently
2 ___ cream cone
3 Exclamation that reads the same forward and backward
4 "___ see ..."
5 Grade that's better than a B-plus: Hyphenated
6 Jack-in-the-___
7 Police officers
8 Plant that excites kittens
9 Things in a museum
10 "Now ___ here!" (outraged cry)
11 ___ of corn
16 Decay
17 "Get ___ of here!"
20 Very fast way to travel

1	2	3	4	■	5	6	7	■	8	9	10	11
12				■	13			■	14			
15				16				17				
■	■	■	18			■	19			■	■	■
20	21	22	■	23		24	■	25		26	27	28
29			30	■	31		32	■	33			
34				35	■	36		37	■	38		
■	■	■	39		40	■	41		42	■	■	■
43	44	45				46				47	48	49
50				■	51			■	52			
53				■	54			■	55			

21 The Tin Woodman's tool
22 Scramble
24 "You've ___ a Friend in Me" (song from "Toy Story")
26 Talk and talk and talk
27 Christmas ___
28 The color at the top of a rainbow
30 The ability to do something well
32 Sport where most players can't touch the ball with their hands
35 Title for a knight
37 Chum
40 Tickle Me ___ (toy based on a "Sesame Street" character)
42 Dogs, cats, fish, and so on
43 Halloween animal
44 Suffix for "Siam"
45 Truck that moves furniture
46 "Thank ___"
47 "Your eyes ___ bigger than your stomach"
48 Move fast
49 Up to this point

27

ACROSS

1 Begin
6 Droop
9 Sleep for an hour or so
12 "Happy Birthday ___": 2 words
13 Long ___ (many years back)
14 It cools down a drink
15 Apply fingerpaints
16 Dover's state: Abbreviation
17 "___ a load of this!"
18 Everest and McKinley: Abbreviation
20 Dr. ___ (rapper who discovered Eminem)
22 It's after Thursday: Abbreviation
25 Mauna ___ (volcano in Hawaii)
27 Strange and spooky
30 There are nine of them in "The Twelve Days of Christmas": 2 words
33 "___ is a terrible thing to waste": 2 words
34 "Yes, ___" (way to agree with a man)
35 "Much ___ About Nothing" (play by William Shakespeare)
36 Yoko ___ (Japanese singer)
37 Tear in two
39 What painters create
41 Solemn promise
44 Loud sounds
48 "What ___ care?" ("Makes no difference to me!"): 2 words
49 Female farm animal
50 Robin Williams played one in "Aladdin"
51 Nickname for a physician
52 TV ___
53 Had a terrible smell

DOWN

1 Cars drive on them: Abbreviation
2 Cat that chased Jerry, in cartoons
3 How sailors say "yes"
4 Wander
5 There are two of them in "The Twelve Days of Christmas": 2 words
6 Not happy
7 It changes on your birthday
8 There are five of them in "The Twelve Days of Christmas": 2 words
9 African country
10 Part of a royal flush

1	2	3	4	5	■	6	7	8	■	9	10	11
12					■	13			■	14		
15					■	16			■	17		
■	■	■	18		19	■	■	20	21		■	■
22	23	24	■	25		26	■	27			28	29
30			31				32					
33					■	34			■	35		
■	■	36			■	■	37		38	■	■	■
39	40		■	41	42	43	■	44		45	46	47
48			■	49			■	50				
51			■	52			■	53				

11 Teacher's ___ (someone the teacher especially likes)
19 Common distress signal
21 ___ room (fun part of a house)
22 Miami's state: Abbreviation
23 ___ into (hit head-on)
24 Very stupid
26 Classified ___ (newspaper section)
28 State next to Illinois: Abbreviation
29 What a vain person has a lot of
31 Days ___ (hotel chain)
32 A breath of fresh ___
38 Person who writes in rhyme
39 Put two and two together
40 Kanga's child
42 It's the O in "I.O.U."
43 Damp
45 ___ bad mood (grouchy): 2 words
46 Something that a religion tells you is bad to do
47 Cry of fear

28

ACROSS

1 Basketball team from Miami
5 Good friend
8 "___, humbug!" (what Scrooge said)
11 Film
12 It's worth 1 or 11 in blackjack
13 Word that's shouted at a bullfight
14 Area in a hospital where surgery takes place: 2 words
17 People write with them
18 "___ good turn deserves another"
19 ___ Sewell ("Black Beauty" author)
20 It means "most" when it's at the end of a word
21 Simple bed
22 Color of broccoli
23 Not thin
24 Insect that likes flowers
25 Drink like a dog: 2 words
28 Covered with water
29 ___ and order (what the police try to maintain)
32 Thing
33 Metal that's just been mined
34 Rival of Nintendo
35 Area in a hospital where babies are born: 2 words
38 Prefix for "historic" or "caution"
39 "___ your age and not your shoe size!"
40 Overhanging parts of a roof
41 "Dear ___" (how to start a letter to a man)
42 "___ whillikers!"
43 Captain Hook's helper

DOWN

1 Wishes
2 Something that happens
3 Puts on TV
4 Iced ___ (cool drink)
5 Artists use it
6 Facial problem for teenagers
7 Lower limb
8 Daniel ___ (American pioneer)
9 Without anyone else
10 Macho guy: Hyphenated

	1	2	3	4		5	6	7		8	9	10
11						12				13		
14					15				16			
17					18				19			
20				21				22				
			23				24					
25	26	27				28				29	30	31
32					33				34			
35				36				37				
38				39				40				
41				42				43				

11 Pout
15 Honk a horn
16 Medium ___ (one way you could order a steak)
21 Bottle ___ (something you have to twist to remove)
22 "Flattery will ___ you nowhere"
23 Give off smoke, or be very angry
24 Red vegetable
25 Has trouble walking
26 Big name in early videogames
27 "Here comes ___ Cottontail ..."
28 Put words on paper
29 Go away
30 Believe the same thing
31 Small bundles
33 First word in a fairy tale
34 Did the backstroke
36 Something to dust with
37 What the French word "oui" means in English

29

ACROSS

1 Oinking animal
4 Class in which you draw
7 Made knots in shoestrings
12 Suffix in some drink names
13 Not high
14 Without other people
15 Area in the game Candy Land: 2 words
18 "Now ___ seen everything!"
19 Fire ___ (stinging insect)
20 It stops a car
23 "Jack fell down and broke ___ crown ..."
24 Eminem's music
27 Use your teeth
28 What jelly comes in
29 Toy that's fun to fly
30 Health ___ (place where people try to get in shape)
31 ___ of gold (what's supposedly at the end of a rainbow)
32 ___ the weather (not feeling well)
33 "___ the Builder" (kids' TV show)
34 Monkey's big relative
35 Area in the game Candy Land: 2 words
42 Inches and miles are ___ of length
43 Equal score for both teams
44 "Skip to My ___"
45 Water birds
46 Animal that purrs
47 Piece of wood in a fireplace

DOWN

1 Friend
2 Wedding phrase: 2 words
3 Stuff that stiffens hair
4 "Wanted dead or ___" (phrase on a Wild West poster)
5 You might skip it in a playground
6 Half of four
7 Green areas around houses
8 More than some: 2 words
9 Sound made by a pigeon
10 Go off the deep ___
11 ___ Moines, Iowa
16 Enjoy
17 Low-ranking hand in poker

1	2	3	■	4	5	6	■	7	8	9	10	11
12			■	13			■	14				
15			16				17					
■	■	■	18			■	19			■	■	■
20	21	22			■	23			■	24	25	26
27				■	28			■	29			
30			■	31			■	32				
■	■	■	33			■	34			■	■	■
35	36	37				38				39	40	41
42					■	43			■	44		
45					■	46			■	47		

20 Pellets in a kid's gun
21 Shred
22 One thing ___ time: 2 words
23 ___ trick (three goals in one soccer game)
24 Get ___ of (remove)
25 Homophone of "eight"
26 Revolutions ___ minute (record's speed)
28 Careers
29 "I ___ this would happen!"
31 Group that tracked down bad guys in the old West
32 Disappointed
33 Have ___ in the belfry (be crazy)
34 Afghanistan's continent
35 ___ shot (photo of a criminal)
36 ___ of a kind (unique)
37 ___ detector
38 Abbreviation that might end a list of things
39 "___ men are created equal"
40 What cows say
41 Dog with a wrinkly face

30

ACROSS

1 Alphabet's beginning
4 Semester
8 What groceries are put into
12 What Homer Simpson says when he does something dumb
13 ___ code (part of a phone number)
14 State with lots of Mormons
15 Health ___ (where some people go to lose weight)
16 Golden-colored drink: 2 words
18 "___ and shine!" ("Get out of bed!")
20 Snooze
21 ___ in the neck (pest)
23 ___ Moines
24 "___ Got the Whole World in His Hands" (song)
27 Brown drink: 2 words
31 "Little Miss Muffet ___ on a tuffet ..."
32 Precious stone
33 Television award
34 What Rembrandt made
35 Group of long, skinny fish
37 Purple drink: 2 words
41 Toymaker at the North Pole
44 Traveled by horse
45 Sand particles
46 First name that could be for either a boy or a girl
47 ___ and reels (fishing equipment)
48 Grains eaten by horses
49 Luthor, to Superman

DOWN

1 They are used to sell things to people
2 Baby ___ (friend of Barney the Dinosaur)
3 Old-time vehicle drawn by horses
4 They show the prices of things
5 It's a Great Lake
6 Stimpy's pal, in cartoons
7 It attracts iron
8 Belch
9 One ___ time (not in groups): 2 words
10 Guy's date
11 "___ Loves You" (Beatles song)
17 At ___ (relaxed, in the military)

1	2	3	■	4	5	6	7	■	8	9	10	11
12			■	13				■	14			
15			■	16				17				
■	■	18	19			■	20			■	■	■
21	22			■	■	23			■	24	25	26
27				28	29				30			
31			■	32			■	■	33			
■	■	■	34			■	35	36			■	■
37	38	39				40			■	41	42	43
44				■	45				■	46		
47				■	48				■	49		

19 "Monsters, ___" (movie with Mike Wazowski)
21 Desktop machines, for short
22 You say it when you realize something
23 What a beaver builds
24 "Every man for ___!" ("No one can get assistance")
25 Kind of tree
26 Where the stars are
28 Shrek is one
29 Releases: 2 words
30 ___ Gibson (famous actor)
34 Big, hairy animals
35 Fix mistakes in writing
36 Gobbles up
37 Sound of a growl
38 Character created by A.A. Milne
39 Opposite of "subtract"
40 "Are you a good witch ___ bad witch?" (line in "The Wizard of Oz"): 2 words
42 Lion in the zodiac
43 "___, fi, fo, fum ..."

31

ACROSS

1 Smack in the face
5 Indicate "good-bye" with your hand
9 Part of a golf course
10 General location
11 Rip ___ Winkle
14 Opposite of "odd"
15 Grime
16 State that's next to Mississippi: Abbreviation
17 The opposite ___ (women, to men)
18 Has a view of
19 Someone who looks down on other people
20 What a red light means
22 ___ machine (invention of Elias Howe)
24 It can delay a baseball game
26 Carbonated drink
27 Part of the alphabet
29 What the daily paper reports
31 ___ and Buster Bunny (characters on "Tiny Toon Adventures")
32 Nearly endless
34 Large pig
36 Portland's state: Abbreviation
37 "What ___ you got to say for yourself?"
38 Stack
39 Large, sturdy tree
40 Where Adam and Eve lived
41 Tiny particle
42 ___ and rave (talk angrily)
43 Not as much

DOWN

1 "That woman is," as a contraction
2 More than likes
3 Host of "Jeopardy!": 2 words
4 Writing instrument
5 Walk in water
6 Zodiac sign that follows Pisces
7 Poems
8 How to stop being hungry

1	2	3	4	■	5	6	7	8	■	■	■	■
9				■	10				■	11	12	13
14				■	15				■	16		
17			■	18				■	19			
■	20		21		■	22		23				■
■	■	24			25	■	26				■	■
■	27					28	■	29			30	■
31				■	32		33		■	34		35
36			■	37				■	38			
39			■	40				■	41			
■	■	■	■	42				■	43			

11 One of the hosts of "Wheel of Fortune": 2 words

12 Easy as falling off ___: 2 words

13 Catch

18 What "expectorate" is a fancy word for

19 Edge

21 Grains fed to horses

23 "What you don't know ___ hurt you"

25 Where Las Vegas is

27 ___ Croft (videogame character)

28 Black bird

30 Songs that are sung by just one person

31 What a ghost says

33 Mailed off

35 Diamonds and rubies, for example

37 Pronoun for a woman

38 Good buddy

32

ACROSS

1 Little devil
4 What a movie director yells to end a scene
7 Carries
12 Summer zodiac sign
13 "Now I see!"
14 In any ___ (no matter what)
15 Insect with black markings on its back
17 Like a dweeb
18 What's left over in a fireplace
19 ___ letter (note that's sent to many people)
20 Where ships come in
23 Race ___ (fast vehicle)
24 "___ a miracle!"
27 Have an ___ for music (be musically talented)
28 Pattern on a leopard
30 Drink that's made from leaves
31 Day before Saturday: Abbreviation
32 You make soup in it
33 What a camper sleeps in
34 Pork ___ (piece of meat)
36 "Cock-a-doodle-___" (rooster's sound)
38 Person who makes bread
40 Insect that lights up
44 Red ___ (serious warning)
45 Hole-in-___ (golfer's goal)
46 Get ___ of (dispose of)
47 Bill ___ (head of Microsoft)
48 Glop
49 Positive response

DOWN

1 Its capital is Springfield: Abbreviation
2 "Give ___ break!": 2 words
3 Like two peas in a ___
4 Taxis
5 Casual way to say "no": Hyphenated
6 Game in which you shout "Not it!"
7 High-voiced male singers
8 "___ the Rainbow" (song in "The Wizard of Oz")
9 Insect that destroys wood
10 Dead-___ street
11 Pig farmer's enclosure

1	2	3	■	4	5	6	■	7	8	9	10	11
12			■	13			■	14				
15			16				■	17				
■	■	■	18			■	19				■	■
20	21	22		■	■	23			■	24	25	26
27			■	28	29				■	30		
31			■	32			■	■	33			
■	■	34	35			■	36	37		■	■	■
38	39				■	40				41	42	43
44					■	45			■	46		
47					■	48			■	49		

16 Large, hairy animal from Asia
19 Pudgy
20 Letters after C
21 Rowing need
22 Insect that chirps
23 You might put a sleeping bag on it
25 Six plus four
26 Rested in a chair
28 Baseball and football, for example
29 Burst a balloon
33 Part of the foot
35 What you say when the teacher takes attendance
36 The Flintstones' pet
37 Black-and-white brand of cookie
38 Let the cat out of the ___ (tell a secret)
39 ___ mode (with ice cream): 2 words
40 Heavy mist
41 Cook bacon
42 Something that isn't true
43 Units of length: Abbreviation

33

ACROSS

1 Jump into a swimming pool
5 Superman wears one
9 Catch forty winks
12 "Hey, what's the big ___?"
13 What the Earth spins on
14 Suffix for "Japan"
15 ___ Groening (creator of "The Simpsons")
16 Part of a big top
17 Take first place
18 Not "he"
19 What W means on a compass
20 "American Idol" host Seacrest
21 Out of ___ (not where it belongs)
23 Extraterrestrial
25 It's inside a basketball
26 Cute ___ button: 2 words
27 Scornful expression
29 Strict
31 Little girl
32 Something that hurts
34 Boar's wife
36 "Come ___ get it!"
37 Smell
38 Coin from Mexico
39 Group at a school: Abbreviation
40 "Out of the frying pan, into the ___"
41 "Roll ___" (command to a dog)
42 "___ cheese!" (photographer's command)
43 ___ of (enjoying)
44 Where a teacher sits in a classroom

DOWN

1 Turns down the lights
2 State that's next to Montana
3 November 11: 2 words
4 Consume
5 Provide the food for a party
6 Tools used for chopping
7 Niña, ___, and Santa Maria (Columbus's ships)

1	2	3	4	■	5	6	7	8	■	9	10	11
12				■	13				■	14		
15				■	16				■	17		
18			■	19				■	20			
■	21		22			■	23	24				■
■	■	25			■	■	■	26			■	■
■	27				28	■	29				30	■
31				■	32	33			■	34		35
36			■	37				■	38			
39			■	40				■	41			
42			■	43				■	44			

8 Word ending that means "most"
9 December 31: 3 words
10 From China or Russia, perhaps
11 Pittsburgh's state: Abbreviation
19 "Those ___ the days"
20 Go up
22 Stops working, like an old motor
24 Not early
27 Christmas figure
28 Item in a car's dashboard
29 Rip into tiny pieces
30 They smell
31 People form them when they sit down
33 Yellow vegetable
35 Labor
37 "Knock it ___!" ("Quit it!")
38 What peas come in

34

ACROSS

1 Famous ___ (brand of cookies)
5 Puts frosting on a cake
9 Big ___ (kind of burger)
12 What a bird builds
13 He built an ark
14 Thin ___ rail: 2 words
15 Mexican snack
16 Measure of land
17 "___ Longstocking" (book)
19 Cost an ___ and a leg (be expensive)
21 ___ King Cole
22 Not crazy
23 Instant ___ (ways to see a sports action again)
25 Baseball players wear them
28 Big boat
29 Containers for oil
32 Dog that's a mix of breeds
35 Aladdin's pet monkey, in the movie
36 Give someone a ___ on the back
37 Less dangerous
38 Part of an album
40 Cast a ballot
42 Orlando's state: Abbreviation
43 $^{1}/_{12}$ of a foot
44 Like the numbers 4, 6, and 8
45 Sneaky
46 Brand of grape soda
47 It grows into a plant

DOWN

1 Prefix for "freeze"
2 "Oh, give ___ home where the buffalo roam ...": 2 words
3 Academy Award
4 Shops
5 ___ trance (hypnotized); 2 words
6 Cold cereal choice: 2 words
7 Before schedule
8 Buildings where tools are kept
9 Charts

■	■	■	■	1	2	3	4	■	5	6	7	8
9	10	11	■	12				■	13			
14			■	15				■	16			
17			18		■	19		20	■	21		
22				■	■	23			24			
■	■	25		26	27	■	28				■	■
29	30					31	■	■	32		33	34
35			■	36			■	37				
38			39	■	40		41		■	42		
43				■	44				■	45		
46				■	47				■	■	■	■

10 Continent next to Europe
11 Cold cereal choice: 2 words
18 Kind of fruit
20 55 ___ (speed limit): Abbreviation
24 ___ beans
26 ___ up (give energy to)
27 People who are forced to work for others
29 Washing tub
30 "... to give her poor dog ___": 2 words
31 You can cook on it
33 Show and ___
34 Hospital food comes on it
37 Button on a fax machine
39 Letters between F and J
41 A golfer puts a ball on one

35

ACROSS

1 Plead
4 What happens in a story
8 Right off the ___ (immediately)
11 Colorful computer made by Apple
13 Strong cord
14 ___ Grande (river)
15 Pink ice cream flavor: 2 words
17 Mischievous child
18 Obedience school command
19 Minor argument
21 Ending for "capital"
24 Cash machine outside a bank: Abbreviation
26 Big-name actor
29 Red-and-white ice cream flavor: 2 words
33 "___, meeny, miney, mo"
34 Golfing organization: Abbreviation
35 Kind of tree
36 Exam
39 Busy ___ beaver: 2 words
41 "Who ___ to say?": 2 words
43 Green ice cream flavor
48 Scary word on Halloween
49 Salt Lake City's state
50 Armored military vehicle
51 Pro and ___ (sides in a debate)
52 "That's ___ problem": 2 words
53 Positive answer

DOWN

1 A baby wears it when eating
2 Flightless Australian bird
3 Chatter on and on
4 Attractive
5 ___ cabin (wooden house)
6 Penguin in the comics
7 What a thermometer measures: Abbreviation
8 Peanut ___ (sweet treat)
9 Point a camera
10 Toy that spins around
12 TV network whose symbol is an eye
16 Person who isn't honest
20 "Do ___ tell you!": 2 words
21 What a glacier is made of

1	2	3			4	5	6	7		8	9	10
11			12		13					14		
15				16						17		
			18				19		20			
21	22	23		24		25			26		27	28
29			30				31	32				
33						34				35		
		36		37	38		39		40			
41	42			43		44				45	46	47
48				49					50			
51				52						53		

22 That female
23 Bring up in conversation
25 Award given to a league's best baseball player of the season: Abbreviation
27 "Money is the root of ___ evil"
28 Animal that represents Aries
30 Deli bread
31 ___ Christie (mystery author)
32 Agency that launches space shuttles: Abbreviation
37 Rotated
38 One of Michael Jackson's brothers
40 Give a performance
41 Letters before D
42 Cow's sound
44 Didn't stand
45 You see stacks of it on farms
46 Ending for "hero"
47 Gives approval to

36

ACROSS

1 Hold ___ (grasp)
5 ___ tea (cold beverage)
9 A bowling ball knocks it down
12 As blind as ___: 2 words
13 Undressed
14 One pal of Winnie-the-Pooh
15 Superhero group that includes the Human Torch and the Thing: 2 words
18 Pinocchio had a large one
19 Stuff that's used to pave a road
20 Name of the prince in the movie "Aladdin"
22 "Ugh!"
24 They connect oxen together
28 Period before Easter
30 The first two-digit number
32 Paste
33 Companies' symbols
35 Shrill bark from a dog
37 Country near England: Abbreviation
38 "___ little teapot ...": 2 words
40 One of the tokens in Monopoly
42 Superhero group that includes Aquaman and Green Lantern: 2 words
48 Remains of a fire
49 Pine or poplar, for example
50 Ring ___ (carnival game)
51 Last name of the author of "Curious George"
52 Gripped
53 Metal fastener

DOWN

1 Big, clumsy person
2 The Lakers' group: Abbreviation
3 Getting browner in the sun
4 Bart Simpson's bus driver
5 Creature with six legs
6 Use a knife
7 Work for a newspaper or magazine
8 Go bad
9 Full-time athlete
10 Evidence of a debt
11 Word that goes with "neither"
16 "___ was saying ...": 2 words
17 Animal that eats flies

1	2	3	4	■	5	6	7	8	■	9	10	11
12				■	13				■	14		
15				16					17			
■	■	18				■	19			■	■	■
20	21		■	22		23	■	24		25	26	27
28			29	■	30		31	■	32			
33				34	■	35		36	■	37		
■	■	■	38		39	■	40		41		■	■
42	43	44				45					46	47
48			■	49				■	50			
51			■	52				■	53			

20 The last word in the Pledge of Allegiance

21 Zodiac sign that comes after Cancer

23 It fits into a lock

25 Enemy on the original "Star Trek"

26 France's continent: Abbreviation

27 ___ the light (understand)

29 "Hop ___!" ("Get moving!"): 2 words

31 Used a hammer

34 Will ___ (actor and rap singer)

36 Prefix for "school" or "teen"

39 Unit of farmland

41 Common grains

42 Mayonnaise holder

43 "What's the ___ in trying?" (quitter's question)

44 Timid

45 Fish that's hard to catch

46 Its capital is Washington, D.C.: Abbreviation

47 Supposed "sixth sense": Abbreviation

37

ACROSS

1 Pigged out
4 A traveler might use one
7 "___ we there yet?"
10 "Do you ___ what I mean?"
11 Part of a book
12 Break the ___ (commit a crime)
13 Toy that you twist
16 King Kong, for example
17 Little baby
18 Set ___ (release)
21 Wager
22 Friend of Bashful and Dopey
25 "___ in a Manger" (Christmas song)
26 Your lungs need it
27 The king of hearts, for example
28 Miles ___ gallon (what MPG stands for)
29 Insect that lives in a hill
30 First name of six U.S. presidents
31 You might put it in a frame
32 Daughter's brother
33 Toy that you crank: Hyphenated
39 When Columbus Day is: Abbreviation
40 Jackie ___ (action star from Hong Kong)
41 ___ good mood (happy): 2 words
42 "You bet!"
43 As ___ as a fox
44 ___ Moines (Iowa city)

DOWN

1 Use a question mark
2 Drink that's often "sweetened" or "unsweetened"
3 Long, wriggly fish
4 Constructed
5 Long ___ (in the past)
6 Bother
7 "I have ___ on my mind": 2 words
8 Popular style of music
9 She's a sheep
11 One of the things Old King Cole called for
14 Not difficult
15 You might sleep on it when you go camping
18 One time around the track course

1	2	3	■	■	4	5	6	■	7	8	9	■
10			■	11				■	12			■
13			14					15				■
■	■	■	16			■	17			■	■	■
18	19	20			■	21			■	22	23	24
25				■	26			■	27			
28			■	29			■	30				
■	■	■	31			■	32			■	■	■
■	33	34				35				36	37	38
■	39			■	40				■	41		
■	42			■	43			■	■	44		

19 "I ___ you one!"
20 It moves a kayak along
21 Little ___ (small amount)
22 It holds back water in a river
23 Raw metal
24 Music purchases, for short
26 Hijinks
27 Walking stick
29 Noah's ___
30 ___ Travolta (movie star)
31 Plays a part
32 Remain in place
33 Happiness
34 It can be worth more than a king
35 The New York Islanders' group: Abbreviation
36 Suggest a price in an auction
37 Last number in a countdown
38 ___ in "xylophone": 2 words

38

ACROSS

1 Small assistant at the North Pole
4 What a boxer punches with
8 Annoying little kid
12 What a tourist to Hawaii wears around the neck
13 ___ in a while (occasionally)
14 Nike's Swoosh, for example
15 Gomez's wife, on "The Addams Family"
17 End of a prayer
18 Electric fish
19 Group of hoops players: Abbreviation
20 Valentines might be trimmed with it
22 At no cost
25 Not later
28 Spring month: Abbreviation
29 Visitor
30 ___ ball (white ball in a game of pool)
31 Body of water
32 Upper limbs
33 What day, month, and year it is
34 Major TV network
36 Child who's a boy
37 Stop sleeping
39 Calvin ___ (former U.S. president)
44 Big animals that look like yaks
45 Bob ___ (man who ran for president against Bill Clinton)
46 Lay down the ___ (explain things firmly)
47 Uncool person
48 Snakes do it to their old skin
49 Homophone of "I"

DOWN

1 Dutch ___ disease (disease of certain trees)
2 Name for a lion
3 Something set off on Independence Day
4 Aluminum ___
5 "Monsters, ___"
6 Biology or chemistry, for example: Abbreviation
7 Brown beverage
8 Tell secrets
9 Something set off on Independence Day: 2 words
10 The Stone ___ (when the Flintstones supposedly lived)

1	2	3	■	4	5	6	7	■	8	9	10	11
12			■	13				■	14			
15			16					■	17			
■	■	18			■	■	■	19			■	■
20	21			■	22	23	24		■	25	26	27
28			■	29					■	30		
31			■	32				■	33			
■	■	34	35		■	■	■	36			■	■
37	38			■	39	40	41				42	43
44				■	45				■	46		
47				■	48				■	49		

11 "It hit me like a ___ of bricks"
16 Wooden item on a golf course
19 You hit a tennis ball over it
20 ___ Vegas (city in Nevada)
21 Gorilla
22 Mink coat, for example
23 Band that sang "Shiny Happy People"
24 Suffix for "priest"
26 Not in
27 Adjective for Willie Winkie
29 It might be unleaded
33 "How ___ look?": 2 words
35 Stoop down
36 You can ride downhill on one
37 Was the champ
38 Big version of a hatchet
39 Music store purchases: Abbreviation
40 ___ and aah (sound impressed)
41 "Hurray" at a bullfight
42 "Don we now our ___ apparel" ("Deck the Halls" line)
43 She gives birth to lambs

39

ACROSS

1 The deepest kind of male voice
5 Homeless wanderer
9 You take a bath in it
12 Former baseball player from Montreal
13 "What's ___ for me?": 2 words
14 ___ Today (popular newspaper)
15 Ownership card in Monopoly
16 Was important
18 "You are what you ___"
20 Get a taste of your ___ medicine
21 What you might call your father
23 Person from the Middle East
27 Cable channel for sports fans
30 "How was ___ know?": 2 words
31 Plumbers work on them
33 Land of leprechauns: Abbreviation
34 A little bit wet
36 It shows everything a restaurant serves
37 "Cat ___ your tongue?"
38 Organ you hear with
40 Fellow
42 It's not a puppy dog: 2 words
47 Umbrellas protect you from it
50 Suffix for "hero"
51 A sword has a sharp one
52 Red Muppet on "Sesame Street"
53 Black stuff used for paving roads
54 "Children should be ___ and not heard" (old saying)
55 Strong ___ ox: 2 words

DOWN

1 Go to ___ (hit the hay)
2 Wood chopper
3 It's on the dashboard of a car
4 Coke or Pepsi, for example
5 That guy
6 Go ___ wild-goose chase: 2 words
7 Not the least ___ (not at all)
8 Boy's name that reads the same forward and backward

1	2	3	4	■	5	6	7	8	■	9	10	11
12				■	13				■	14		
15				■	16				17			
■	■	18		19	■	■	■	20			■	■
21	22		■	23	24	25	26	■	27		28	29
30			■	31				32	■	33		
34			35	■	36				■	37		
■	■	38		39	■	■	■	40	41		■	■
42	43				44	45	46	■	47		48	49
50			■	51				■	52			
53			■	54				■	55			

9 They're on the back of a car: 2 words
10 Make ___ of (put to work)
11 Evil
17 Partner of a ram
19 Poke someone on the shoulder
21 "___ I say that?"
22 ___ standstill (not moving): 2 words
24 Part of a basketball hoop
25 Baboon's relative
26 Big ___ (landmark in London)
28 Athlete who gets paid
29 Butterfly catcher
32 Grand total
35 Touch gently
39 Dark-colored breads
41 Territory
42 First-aid ___
43 "... and a partridge ___ pear tree": 2 words
44 Letters after B
45 Get older
46 Number of years in a decade
48 "___ Yankee Doodle Dandy": 2 words
49 Prefix for "smoking" or "profit"

40

ACROSS

1 "Don't ___ all your eggs in one basket"
4 Part of a constellation
8 Ending for "gang" or "young"
12 Magilla Gorilla, for example
13 "Yes ___?": 2 words
14 Batman or Superman, for example
15 "This ___ surprise!": 2 words
16 Last test before summer vacation: 2 words
18 Button you press in a bowling alley
20 "___ little teapot, short and stout ...": 2 words
21 Hungry ___ bear: 2 words
22 Food containing meat and potatoes: 2 words
23 Snaky fish
24 Politician in Congress: Abbreviation
25 Ending for "lion"
28 Apply softly, like makeup
30 "That's ___, folks!"
33 Good friend
35 "What time ___?": 2 words
39 Sign that comes before Virgo
40 Ginger ___
41 Country that's shaped like a boot
42 Smith and Jones, for two: 2 words
45 Peak
46 Level
47 It grows on the north side of trees
48 "___ never been so insulted in all my life!"
49 Home in a tree
50 Word you use during long division
51 Neighbor of Homer, on "The Simpsons"

DOWN

1 Groups of two
2 Angry
3 Poke fun at
4 Not hard
5 Prefix that means "three"
6 Musical that includes the song "Tomorrow"
7 Wandered around
8 This girl
9 The third-largest state

1	2	3	■	4	5	6	7	■	8	9	10	11
12			■	13				■	14			
15			■	16				17				
18			19		■	20			■	21		
22				■	■	23			■	24		
■	■	■	25	26	27	■	28		29	■	■	■
30	31	32	■	33		34	■	■	35	36	37	38
39			■	40			■	41				
42			43				44		■	45		
46				■	47				■	48		
49				■	50				■	51		

10 Get rid of chalk marks
11 Person from the capital of 41-Across
17 Sounds that come after "tra" in a song: 2 words
19 A shepherd might take care of her
26 Have a short attention ___
27 Salty lunch meat
29 ___-O-Honey (kind of candy)
30 Woody ___ (famous movie director)
31 "___ me alone!"
32 Comes in last place in a race
34 Yellow fruit
36 Soft fabric
37 "___ Lucy" (old sitcom): 2 words
38 Used a keyboard
41 "This ___ sudden!": 2 words
43 Explosive material: Abbreviation
44 Suffix that can make "smart" mean "most smart"

ANSWERS

1

C	U	T	■	B	E	D	■	B	I	K	E	R
U	S	A	■	A	Y	E	■	A	L	I	V	E
P	E	N	N	I	E	S	■	N	A	M	E	D
■	■	G	E	T	S	■	S	K	Y	■	■	■
M	I	L	E	■	■	F	E	E	■	S	O	S
O	N	E	D	O	L	L	A	R	B	I	L	L
M	A	D	■	M	A	Y	■	■	A	N	D	Y
■	■	■	H	E	S	■	W	A	R	N	■	■
M	O	R	A	L	■	N	I	C	K	E	L	S
A	W	A	R	E	■	A	S	H	■	R	I	O
T	E	M	P	T	■	G	E	E	■	S	P	Y

2

I	D	O	L	■	O	N	C	E	■	H	I	P
N	O	N	O	■	C	O	O	P	■	A	L	E
C	H	A	R	L	E	S	S	C	H	U	L	Z
■	■	■	D	O	A	■	T	O	O	N	■	■
I	T	S	■	T	N	T	■	T	O	T	A	L
C	A	M	P	■	S	E	E	■	D	E	L	I
K	N	E	E	S	■	N	A	P	■	D	I	D
■	■	L	E	A	D	■	S	I	P	■	■	■
B	I	L	L	W	A	T	T	E	R	S	O	N
A	C	E	■	E	R	I	E	■	O	H	I	O
R	E	D	■	D	E	E	R	■	M	E	L	T

3

C	A	R	■	I	M	P	■	C	O	L	T	S
A	P	E	■	D	I	E	■	O	M	A	H	A
P	U	P	T	E	N	T	■	M	I	N	E	D
■	■	H	A	T	■	M	I	T	T	■	■	■
L	A	C	E	S	■	D	O	C	■	E	W	E
I	C	A	N	■	W	O	W	■	G	R	A	Y
P	E	N	■	W	I	G	■	R	A	N	G	E
■	■	■	T	H	I	N	■	S	O	S	■	■
S	T	E	A	L	■	C	O	M	P	A	S	S
A	R	E	N	T	■	A	S	A	■	I	K	E
G	A	N	G	S	■	T	O	N	■	R	Y	E

4

M	A	C	■	A	B	E	L	■	S	T	A	G
A	S	H	■	R	U	L	E	■	L	E	G	O
T	I	E	■	E	M	M	A	■	Y	A	R	N
E	D	E	N	■	M	E	N	U	■	M	E	G
■	E	R	A	S	E	R	■	S	A	M	E	■
■	■	L	I	A	R	■	S	E	G	A	■	■
■	S	E	L	L	■	S	T	R	E	S	S	■
A	H	A	■	T	A	P	E	■	S	C	A	M
M	A	D	E	■	C	A	V	E	■	O	U	I
E	V	E	N	■	E	R	I	E	■	T	N	T
N	E	R	D	■	S	E	E	K	■	S	A	T

5

D	E	C	■	A	H	A	■	■	C	H	U	G
I	L	L	■	S	E	M	I	■	H	O	S	E
S	K	I	■	P	R	I	N	C	I	P	A	L
■	■	M	A	C	■	■	F	A	N	■	■	■
L	I	B	R	A	R	I	A	N	■	U	P	S
I	T	E	M	■	E	T	C	■	I	N	T	O
P	E	R	■	C	U	S	T	O	D	I	A	N
■	■	■	A	B	S	■	■	G	O	T	■	■
C	O	U	N	S	E	L	O	R	■	I	S	A
A	U	N	T	■	D	A	N	E	■	N	E	D
P	R	O	S	■	■	Y	E	S	■	G	A	S

6

R	A	C	K	■	L	I	E	■	S	M	E	E
I	R	A	N	■	I	V	Y	■	T	I	E	S
P	E	P	E	■	T	E	E	■	A	S	K	S
■	■	T	E	S	T	■	S	L	I	T	■	■
A	T	A	■	E	L	F	■	O	R	E	O	S
D	O	I	■	N	E	A	T	O	■	R	A	P
S	O	N	G	S	■	T	I	S	■	S	K	Y
■	■	K	N	E	W	■	D	E	P	P	■	■
A	S	I	A	■	A	L	I	■	T	O	A	D
S	O	R	T	■	S	E	E	■	A	C	M	E
I	N	K	S	■	H	E	R	■	S	K	I	N

7

W	A	S	P	S		O	A	R		A	U	G
A	T	A	R	I		L	I	E		U	S	A
R	E	L	A	X		D	R	E	S	S	E	S
		E	Y	E	S		S	K	I	T		
H	I	M		S	I	N		S	N	I	P	S
A	T	O	P		T	O	M		K	N	E	E
S	T	R	A	Y		D	O	C		T	A	X
		E	W	E	S		P	O	L	E		
D	O	G	S	L	E	D		M	I	X	E	S
U	N	O		L	E	O		E	R	A	S	E
D	A	N		O	K	S		T	A	S	T	E

8

P	I	G		S	E	A		R	A	D	A	R
A	T	A		H	A	N		A	R	O	S	E
C	A	R	P	O	R	T		R	E	L	A	X
		T	I	E	S		M	E	A	L		
A	C	H	E	S		W	A	R		Y	E	S
S	U	B	S		D	O	T		S	P	A	T
H	E	R		C	O	W		C	H	A	T	S
		O	B	O	E		P	O	O	R		
B	O	O	E	D		C	L	U	T	T	E	R
A	N	K	L	E		O	A	R		O	W	E
T	E	S	T	S		T	N	T		N	E	D

9

L	A	M	P	S		J	U	G		P	A	Y
A	G	A	I	N		A	T	E		I	C	E
W	O	R	S	E		Y	A	N	K	E	E	S
		L	A	R	K		H	E	N			
A	M	I		T	I	P		S	O	R	E	S
S	O	N	G		D	O	G		T	O	G	O
A	E	S	O	P		P	U	T		C	O	B
			N	E	T		M	I	L	K		
D	O	D	G	E	R	S		B	A	I	T	S
O	N	E		L	I	E		E	V	E	N	T
T	A	N		S	O	W		T	A	S	T	Y

10

A	L	S	O		S	A	G	S		D	E	N
B	E	T	H		N	O	N	O		I	V	E
C	O	U	N	T	O	L	A	F		S	E	W
			O	H	O		T	A	I	L		
I	F	S		A	P	E			N	I	N	A
L	E	M	O	N	Y	S	N	I	C	K	E	T
L	E	A	N			S	I	T		E	G	O
		R	A	I	N		E	S	T			
R	A	T		J	I	M	C	A	R	R	E	Y
U	S	E		K	N	E	E		I	O	W	A
B	A	R		L	E	T	S		P	O	E	M

11

G	O	D		C	A	B	S		S	T	A	G
A	P	E		A	T	O	P		H	O	M	E
V	E	N	T	N	O	R	A	V	E	N	U	E
E	R	I	E		M	I	C	E		E	S	S
L	A	M	E	R		S	E	N		S	E	E
			N	A	G		S	U	M			
M	A	T		B	I	D		S	O	N	A	R
I	T	O		B	A	I	T		L	E	N	O
M	A	R	V	I	N	G	A	R	D	E	N	S
E	L	S	E		T	I	M	E		D	I	E
S	L	O	T		S	T	E	P		Y	E	S

12

G	A	B		S	L	E	D		P	A	P	A
U	S	E		P	I	L	E		A	G	E	D
T	H	E	J	E	F	F	E	R	S	O	N	S
			O	N	E		J	E	T			
B	O	W	E	D		M	A	D		Z	I	P
A	W	A	Y		P	A	Y		T	I	D	E
T	E	X		S	I	X		T	U	T	O	R
			A	I	R		T	U	T			
T	H	E	B	R	A	D	Y	B	U	N	C	H
A	B	E	L		T	A	P	E		B	O	O
P	O	L	E		E	Y	E	S		A	P	E

13

H	A	R	M			B	A	D		G	I	S
I	C	E	U	P		A	P	U		E	V	E
P	E	P	S	I		N	E	D		T	E	A
			H	A	H	A		E	A	R		
B	A	R		N	U	N	S		R	E	S	T
C	H	O	C	O	L	A	T	E	C	A	K	E
D	A	T	A		A	S	I	N		L	I	E
		A	R	M		P	R	E	Y			
J	E	T		E	E	L		M	E	A	N	S
O	W	E		A	S	I		Y	A	B	B	A
Y	E	S		L	E	T			R	E	A	D

14

S	E	A	N		A	D	S		P	E	R	M
E	G	G	O		B	A	A		A	S	I	A
W	O	O	D	R	O	W	W	I	L	S	O	N
			D	A	Y		Y	A	M			
S	H	E	E	P		H	E	M		L	E	G
H	O	L	D		C	A	R		C	A	N	E
E	E	K		A	R	T		D	O	D	G	E
			I	D	O		M	O	O			
A	N	D	R	E	W	J	A	C	K	S	O	N
Y	O	Y	O		D	O	T		E	U	R	O
E	V	E	N		S	E	E		D	E	E	R

15

D	U	H		S	N	A	G		S	H	I	P
O	F	A		C	O	P	E		C	O	D	E
H	O	T	W	A	T	E	R		A	T	O	Z
			A	R	E		B	A	T	H		
A	C	H	Y			B	I	D		E	A	R
R	O	O		M	E	A	L	S		A	T	E
T	O	T		A	I	R			A	D	A	M
		D	O	N	T		S	I	S			
S	O	O	N		H	O	T	S	H	O	T	S
U	R	G	E		E	R	I	E		W	E	E
M	E	S	S		R	A	R	E		L	A	W

16

				P	A	S	T		A	B	C	S
F	I	R		A	L	P	O		C	A	L	L
I	D	A		D	I	E	T		T	R	E	E
L	E	G	S		E	W	E	S		B	A	D
L	A	G	O	O	N	S		C	O	I	N	S
		E	A	R	S		M	A	K	E		
A	N	D	R	E		P	A	R	A	D	E	S
T	O	Y		O	V	E	R		Y	O	R	K
L	O	A	N		E	A	T	S		L	I	E
A	N	N	O		A	C	H	E		L	E	E
S	E	N	T		L	E	A	N				

17

D	A	D		T	E	A		P	A	P	E	R
I	C	E		W	A	R		O	L	I	V	E
D	E	N	T	I	S	T		T	O	T	E	D
			E	N	T		P	A	T			
I	D	E	A			C	A	T		M	A	P
D	E	R	M	A	T	O	L	O	G	I	S	T
O	W	N		M	O	W			A	S	I	A
			C	U	P		P	A	N			
G	A	T	E	S		S	U	R	G	E	O	N
A	L	O	N	E		A	R	M		E	W	E
P	I	N	T	S		D	R	Y		L	E	T

18

S	A	L	E	M		L	I	L		B	A	G
A	L	I	V	E		A	M	I		L	I	E
D	A	T	E	D		D	A	B		A	R	M
		T	R	A	P		C	R	O	C		
C	A	L		L	O	T		A	N	K	L	E
D	R	E	W		P	O	W		A	B	E	L
S	E	W	E	D		M	A	P		E	E	K
		O	B	O	E		R	E	B	A		
J	A	M		U	V	W		T	R	U	M	P
E	Y	E		S	E	E		E	A	T	E	R
T	E	N		E	N	D		S	T	Y	L	E

19

A	B	C	■	W	A	S	■	A	S	I	A	■
P	E	A	■	A	L	I	■	E	A	R	N	■
E	L	V	I	S	P	R	E	S	L	E	Y	■
■	■	E	C	H	O	■	D	O	E	■	■	■
H	O	M	E	Y	■	D	I	P	■	M	A	T
I	W	A	S	■	B	A	T	■	S	O	L	O
T	E	N	■	M	A	Y	■	H	O	N	E	Y
■	■	■	F	O	R	■	F	A	D	S	■	■
■	F	R	A	N	K	S	I	N	A	T	R	A
■	R	U	L	E	■	A	N	D	■	E	A	R
■	O	N	L	Y	■	Y	E	S	■	R	Y	E

20

C	A	R	S	■	R	A	G	■	S	C	A	T
A	B	A	T	■	I	D	O	■	P	O	G	O
P	E	T	E	■	C	D	S	■	I	T	E	M
■	■	T	A	L	E	■	P	A	N	T	■	■
B	E	L	L	E	■	L	E	I	■	O	F	A
O	W	E	■	M	A	I	L	S	■	N	E	D
Y	E	S	■	O	R	E	■	L	A	M	B	S
■	■	N	O	N	E	■	V	E	T	O	■	■
T	R	A	P	■	T	W	O	■	B	U	D	S
H	I	K	E	■	H	A	T	■	A	T	I	T
E	D	E	N	■	A	X	E	■	T	H	E	Y

21

22

O	C	E	A	N	■	S	A	P	■	L	A	D
F	R	A	M	E	■	P	I	E	■	O	W	E
F	A	T	A	L	B	E	R	T	■	R	A	N
E	V	E	■	S	U	E	■	S	T	A	R	T
R	E	N	■	O	D	D	S	■	A	X	E	S
■	■	■	A	N	D	■	A	U	G	■	■	■
S	H	O	T	■	Y	A	R	N	■	A	R	M
L	E	P	E	W	■	S	A	W	■	S	E	A
A	R	E	■	H	E	Y	H	E	Y	H	E	Y
T	E	N	■	O	N	O	■	L	O	O	S	E
E	S	S	■	S	T	U	■	L	O	W	E	R

23

24

25

D	I	P	S	■	P	O	S	T	■	F	E	E
U	T	A	H	■	A	N	T	I	■	A	T	E
D	O	D	O	■	D	E	A	D	L	O	C	K
■	■	L	E	A	D	■	B	Y	A	■	■	■
R	O	O	■	S	E	C	■	■	S	W	I	G
I	N	C	■	A	D	O	R	E	■	A	C	E
O	A	K	S	■	■	D	O	G	■	R	Y	E
■	■	■	I	A	M	■	C	O	A	L	■	■
S	H	E	R	L	O	C	K	■	P	O	G	S
T	O	N	■	L	O	N	E	■	E	C	H	O
Y	E	T	■	I	S	N	T	■	S	K	I	P

26

D	I	A	L	■	A	B	C	■	C	A	S	E
A	C	H	E	■	M	O	O	■	A	R	E	A
B	E	A	T	R	I	X	P	O	T	T	E	R
■	■	■	S	O	N	■	S	U	N	■	■	■
J	A	M	■	T	U	G	■	T	I	G	E	R
E	X	I	T	■	S	O	S	■	P	A	V	E
T	E	X	A	S	■	T	O	P	■	B	E	D
■	■	■	L	I	E	■	C	A	P	■	■	■
B	E	V	E	R	L	Y	C	L	E	A	R	Y
A	S	A	N	■	M	O	E	■	T	R	U	E
T	E	N	T	■	O	U	R	■	S	E	N	T

27

S	T	A	R	T	■	S	A	G	■	N	A	P
T	O	Y	O	U	■	A	G	O	■	I	C	E
S	M	E	A	R	■	D	E	L	■	G	E	T
■	■	■	M	T	S	■	■	D	R	E	■	■
F	R	I	■	L	O	A	■	E	E	R	I	E
L	A	D	I	E	S	D	A	N	C	I	N	G
A	M	I	N	D	■	S	I	R	■	A	D	O
■	■	■	O	N	O	■	■	R	I	P	■	■
A	R	T	■	V	O	W	■	N	O	I	S	E
D	O	I	■	E	W	E	■	G	E	N	I	E
D	O	C	■	S	E	T	■	S	T	A	N	K

28

■	H	E	A	T	■	P	A	L	■	B	A	H
M	O	V	I	E	■	A	C	E	■	O	L	E
O	P	E	R	A	T	I	N	G	R	O	O	M
P	E	N	S	■	O	N	E	■	A	N	N	A
E	S	T	■	C	O	T	■	G	R	E	E	N
■	■	■	F	A	T	■	B	E	E	■	■	■
L	A	P	U	P	■	W	E	T	■	L	A	W
I	T	E	M	■	O	R	E	■	S	E	G	A
M	A	T	E	R	N	I	T	Y	W	A	R	D
P	R	E	■	A	C	T	■	E	A	V	E	S
S	I	R	■	G	E	E	■	S	M	E	E	■

29

P	I	G	■	A	R	T	■	L	A	C	E	D
A	D	E	■	L	O	W	■	A	L	O	N	E
L	O	L	L	I	P	O	P	W	O	O	D	S
■	■	■	I	V	E	■	A	N	T	■	■	■
B	R	A	K	E	■	H	I	S	■	R	A	P
B	I	T	E	■	J	A	R	■	K	I	T	E
S	P	A	■	P	O	T	■	U	N	D	E	R
■	■	■	B	O	B	■	A	P	E	■	■	■
M	O	L	A	S	S	E	S	S	W	A	M	P
U	N	I	T	S	■	T	I	E	■	L	O	U
G	E	E	S	E	■	C	A	T	■	L	O	G

30

A	B	C	■	T	E	R	M	■	B	A	G	S
D	O	H	■	A	R	E	A	■	U	T	A	H
S	P	A	■	G	I	N	G	E	R	A	L	E
■	■	■	R	I	S	E	■	N	A	P	■	■
P	A	I	N	■	■	D	E	S	■	H	E	S
C	H	O	C	O	L	A	T	E	M	I	L	K
S	A	T	■	G	E	M	■	■	E	M	M	Y
■	■	■	A	R	T	■	E	E	L	S	■	■
G	R	A	P	E	S	O	D	A	■	E	L	F
R	O	D	E	■	G	R	I	T	■	L	E	E
R	O	D	S	■	O	A	T	S	■	F	O	E

31

S	L	A	P		W	A	V	E				
H	O	L	E		A	R	E	A		V	A	N
E	V	E	N		D	I	R	T		A	L	A
S	E	X		S	E	E	S		S	N	O	B
	S	T	O	P		S	E	W	I	N	G	
		R	A	I	N		S	O	D	A		
	L	E	T	T	E	R		N	E	W	S	
B	A	B	S		V	A	S	T		H	O	G
O	R	E		H	A	V	E		P	I	L	E
O	A	K		E	D	E	N		A	T	O	M
				R	A	N	T		L	E	S	S

32

I	M	P		C	U	T		T	O	T	E	S
L	E	O		A	H	A		E	V	E	N	T
L	A	D	Y	B	U	G		N	E	R	D	Y
			A	S	H		F	O	R	M		
D	O	C	K			C	A	R		I	T	S
E	A	R		S	P	O	T	S		T	E	A
F	R	I		P	O	T			T	E	N	T
		C	H	O	P		D	O	O			
B	A	K	E	R		F	I	R	E	F	L	Y
A	L	E	R	T		O	N	E		R	I	D
G	A	T	E	S		G	O	O		Y	E	S

33

D	I	V	E		C	A	P	E		N	A	P
I	D	E	A		A	X	I	S		E	S	E
M	A	T	T		T	E	N	T		W	I	N
S	H	E		W	E	S	T		R	Y	A	N
	O	R	D	E	R		A	L	I	E	N	
		A	I	R				A	S	A		
	S	N	E	E	R		S	T	E	R	N	
L	A	S	S		A	C	H	E		S	O	W
A	N	D		O	D	O	R		P	E	S	O
P	T	A		F	I	R	E		O	V	E	R
S	A	Y		F	O	N	D		D	E	S	K

34

				A	M	O	S		I	C	E	S
M	A	C		N	E	S	T		N	O	A	H
A	S	A		T	A	C	O		A	C	R	E
P	I	P	P	I		A	R	M		O	L	D
S	A	N	E			R	E	P	L	A	Y	S
		C	A	P	S		S	H	I	P		
B	A	R	R	E	L	S			M	U	T	T
A	B	U		P	A	T		S	A	F	E	R
S	O	N	G		V	O	T	E		F	L	A
I	N	C	H		E	V	E	N		S	L	Y
N	E	H	I		S	E	E	D				

35

B	E	G			P	L	O	T		B	A	T
I	M	A	C		R	O	P	E		R	I	O
B	U	B	B	L	E	G	U	M		I	M	P
			S	I	T		S	P	A	T		
I	S	M	A	T	M				S	T	A	R
C	H	E	R	R	Y	V	A	N	I	L	L	A
E	E	N	Y			P	G	A		E	L	M
		T	E	S	T		A	S	A			
A	M	I		P	I	S	T	A	C	H	I	O
B	O	O		U	T	A	H		T	A	N	K
C	O	N		N	O	T	A			Y	E	S

36

O	N	T	O		I	C	E	D		P	I	N
A	B	A	T		N	U	D	E		R	O	O
F	A	N	T	A	S	T	I	C	F	O	U	R
		N	O	S	E		T	A	R			
A	L	I		I	C	K		Y	O	K	E	S
L	E	N	T		T	E	N		G	L	U	E
L	O	G	O	S		Y	A	P		I	R	E
			I	M	A		I	R	O	N		
J	U	S	T	I	C	E	L	E	A	G	U	E
A	S	H		T	R	E	E		T	O	S	S
R	E	Y		H	E	L	D		S	N	A	P

37

A	T	E			M	A	P		A	R	E	
S	E	E		P	A	G	E		L	A	W	
K	A	L	E	I	D	O	S	C	O	P	E	
			A	P	E		T	O	T			
L	O	O	S	E		B	E	T		D	O	C
A	W	A	Y		A	I	R		C	A	R	D
P	E	R		A	N	T		J	A	M	E	S
			A	R	T		S	O	N			
	J	A	C	K	I	N	T	H	E	B	O	X
	O	C	T		C	H	A	N		I	N	A
	Y	E	S		S	L	Y			D	E	S

38

E	L	F		F	I	S	T		B	R	A	T
L	E	I		O	N	C	E		L	O	G	O
M	O	R	T	I	C	I	A		A	M	E	N
		E	E	L				N	B	A		
L	A	C	E		F	R	E	E		N	O	W
A	P	R		G	U	E	S	T		C	U	E
S	E	A		A	R	M	S		D	A	T	E
		C	B	S				S	O	N		
W	A	K	E		C	O	O	L	I	D	G	E
O	X	E	N		D	O	L	E		L	A	W
N	E	R	D		S	H	E	D		E	Y	E

39

B	A	S	S		H	O	B	O		T	U	B
E	X	P	O		I	N	I	T		U	S	A
D	E	E	D		M	A	T	T	E	R	E	D
		E	A	T				O	W	N		
D	A	D		A	R	A	B		E	S	P	N
I	T	O		P	I	P	E	S		I	R	E
D	A	M	P		M	E	N	U		G	O	T
		E	A	R				M	A	N		
K	I	T	T	Y	C	A	T		R	A	I	N
I	N	E		E	D	G	E		E	L	M	O
T	A	R		S	E	E	N		A	S	A	N

40

P	U	T		S	T	A	R		S	T	E	R
A	P	E		O	R	N	O		H	E	R	O
I	S	A		F	I	N	A	L	E	X	A	M
R	E	S	E	T		I	M	A		A	S	A
S	T	E	W			E	E	L		S	E	N
			E	S	S		D	A	B			
A	L	L		P	A	L			I	S	I	T
L	E	O		A	L	E		I	T	A	L	Y
L	A	S	T	N	A	M	E	S		T	O	P
E	V	E	N		M	O	S	S		I	V	E
N	E	S	T		I	N	T	O		N	E	D

ABOUT THE AUTHOR

Trip Payne is a professional puzzlemaker living in Boca Raton, Florida. He made his first puzzles when he was in elementary school, had his first puzzle in a national magazine when he was in junior high, and worked for a major puzzle magazine when he was in college.

He has made kids' puzzles for such places as *Scholastic News*, *Games Junior*, and *TV Guide*, and is a three-time winner of the American Crossword Puzzle Tournament. This is his eighth book in the "Crosswords for Kids" series for Sterling Publishing.

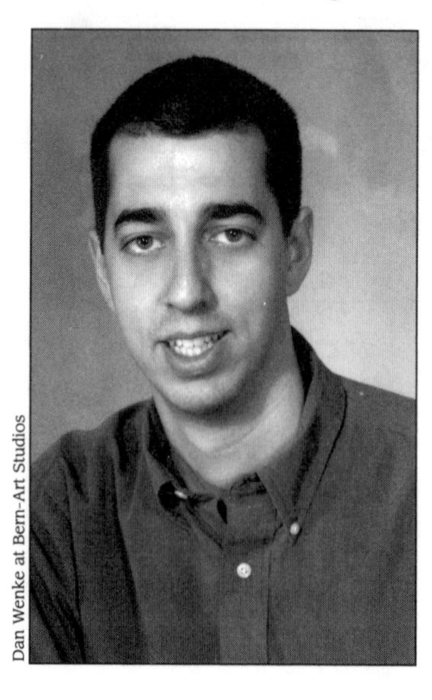

Dan Wenke at Bern-Art Studios

WHAT IS MENSA?

Mensa
The High IQ Society

Mensa is the international society for people with a high IQ. We have more than 100,000 members in over 40 countries worldwide.

The society's aims are:
- to identify and foster human intelligence for the benefit of humanity;
- to encourage research in the nature, characteristics, and uses of intelligence;
- to provide a stimulating intellectual and social environment for its members.

Anyone with an IQ score in the top two percent of population is eligible to become a member of Mensa—are you the "one in 50" we've been looking for?

Mensa membership offers an excellent range of benefits:
- Networking and social activities nationally and around the world;
- Special Interest Groups (hundreds of chances to pursue your hobbies and interests—from art to zoology!);
- Monthly International Journal, national magazines, and regional newsletters;

- Local meetings—from game challenges to food and drink;
- National and international weekend gatherings and conferences;
- Intellectually stimulating lectures and seminars;
- Access to the worldwide SIGHT network for travelers and hosts.

For more information about Mensa International:
www.mensa.org
Mensa International
15 The Ivories
6–8 Northampton Street
Islington, London N1 2HY
United Kingdom

For more information about American Mensa:
www.us.mensa.org
Telephone: (817) 607-0060
American Mensa Ltd.
1229 Corporate Drive West
Arlington, TX 76006-6103 USA

For more information about British Mensa (UK and Ireland):
www.mensa.org.uk
Telephone: +44 (0) 1902 772771
E-mail: enquiries@mensa.org.uk
British Mensa Ltd.
St. John's House
St. John's Square
Wolverhampton WV2 4AH
United Kingdom

For more information about Australian Mensa:
www.au.mensa.org
Telephone: +61 1902 260 594
E-mail: info@au.mensa.org
Australian Mensa Inc.
PO Box 212
Darlington WA 6070 Australia